Daylilies

THE PERFECT PERENNIAL

Lewis and Nancy Hill

Text Photographs by Darrel Apps

Illustrations by Robin D. Brickman

A Garden Way Publishing Book

Storey Communications, Inc.
Schoolhouse Road
Pownal, Vermont 05261

Cover, interior design, and production by Cindy McFarland

Edited by Gwen W. Steege

Front and back cover photographs by Derek Fell

Illustrations by Robin D. Brickman except
pages 91-95 by Judy Eliason

Text and cover printed by Courier

Color text printed by Baronet Litho

Third Printing, February 1992

Printed in the United States

Library of Congress Cataloging-in-Publication Data
Hill, Lewis, 1924-
   Daylilies : the perfect perennial / Lewis Hill, Nancy Hill.
     p. cm.
   "A Garden Way Publishing book"
   Includes index.
   ISBN 0-88266-652-5 : $24.95. -- ISBN 0-88266-651-7 (pbk.) : $14.95
    1. Daylilies.   I. Hill, Nancy.   II. Title.
SB413.D3H55 1991   90-55607
635.9'34324--dc20   CIP

C O N T E N T S

About the Authors

Lewis Hill began growing daylilies in the late 1940s, when he established a small plant nursery in northern Vermont where his Yankee ancestors settled 200 years ago. Besides daylily species and early cultivars, he grew a variety of hardy plants, small fruits, antique apples, greenhouse plants, and Christmas trees. When the hefty Vermont snows buried the plants, he lectured and wrote books and articles on those subjects. He helped form the Vermont Plantsmen's Association and later served as president. He shared his forestry and gardening knowledge with nearly 200 young people as leader of a 4-H club for thirty years.

Nancy Hill, when she joined Lewis and the firm in 1969, was a teacher fresh from a two-year assignment in Thailand and had never planted a seed or pruned a twig. She soon became an enthusiastic gardener, however, and together they agreed that daylilies were the ideal plants to fill the vacuum left when they sold their Hillcrest Nursery in 1981. Vermont Daylilies, their present business, was born and has grown to over 500 cultivars, including some of their own introductions. Considering the Hills' enthusiasm for the daylily, and its immense popularity, it seemed only natural that they felt the urge to write a book about their favorite plant.

About the Photographer

Darrel Apps, who provided all of the interior photographs, first became fascinated with daylilies when, as a 10 year old, he admired daylilies growing under the eaves of his one-room schoolhouse near Wild Rose, Wisconsin. Years later, he grew his first daylilies from seed purchased from an English mail-order catalog. When they bloomed, he experienced his first and only disappointment with the genus — as he put it, "They were uglier than sin!" The secret he was soon to learn was that the best daylilies in the world were produced by hybridizers in the United States. After receiving a Ph.D. in horticulture at the University of Wisconsin, Apps taught at both the University of Kentucky and Penn State University, where he and Dr. Charles Heuser created the first daylily propagated by tissue culture. To date, Apps has forty-two cultivars to his credit. He has published articles on daylilies for several professional journals, and wrote the Introduction to the 1986 revision of Stout's *Daylilies*. In 1984, he joined the United States National Arboretum to collect plants in Korea. After heading the Department of Education at Longwood Gardens for seventeen years, Apps left in 1987 to start his own horticulture consulting business, Garden Adventures, and to operate a mail-order daylily business, Woodside.

➜ *Acknowledgements* ←

We are grateful to the following individuals and organizations for the information and other assistance they have provided: Sinclair Adam; The American Hemerocallis Society; *The Daylily Journal* and its editor Frances Gatlin; Leonard Perry; Flora Philbrook; and the Gilbert H. Wild and Son, Inc. daylily nursery.
We appreciate the beautiful illustrations drawn by Robin Brickman, and Derek Fell's cover photographs.
We also want to thank Cindy McFarland, the book's designer; and especially our editor, Gwen Steege, for her patience and tremendous assistance.

Introduction

WHEN WE MENTIONED to a friend that we were writing a book on growing daylilies, he remarked, "What can you say? You don't need any instructions to grow daylilies. They just grow by themselves."

He had a good point. The old Lemon Lily that surrounded many homesteads in the last century, the tawny Europa that escaped from gardens and spread along the roadsides like wildfire, and the early golden Middendorff grow with no help from anyone. Those, along with many equally vigorous early hybrids, were the daylilies we started to grow in 1947, because they were the only ones available. When we tried to get rid of these energetic plants a few decades later, in order to replace them with the newer kinds, we had a terrible time. We tried smothering them with plastic, used various weedkillers, plowed them under, buried them with soil, dumped strong fertilizer over them, and still it took several years before the last sprout gave up. We felt a lot like the Australian who bought a new boomer-

ang and couldn't throw away the old one.

The friend who thought we shouldn't waste our time writing a book wasn't aware that over 32,000 new named daylilies have been created in every size, shape, color, form, and height imaginable, many in the past two decades. The ancient Oriental wildflower has been converted into a most remarkable herbaceous perennial. All of these new Cinderella-like transformations are not as completely carefree as their ancestors, but compared to many other plants, they can still be classified as easy-care. As long as we select each new acquisition carefully, to be sure it will survive in our climate, and we are careful to plant it properly, provide the soil, exposure, and fertilizer it likes best, and divide it occasionally, our daylilies flourish. Our collection now consists of over 500 cultivars, which we never need to stake and practically never spray.

Probably our friend wasn't aware as well, of all the interesting things about the daylily that most people don't know: its history, uses as a medicine or food, and all the different wild species there are that grow all over the Orient. He likely wasn't aware, as we weren't a few years ago, of the many different types that are available now: double, fragrant, miniature, ruffled, spider, and trumpet-shaped flowers, as well as those with halos, blotches, and "piecrust" edgings.

The rewards our daylily plants shower on us far outweigh the minimal care we give them. Their beauty, length of bloom, longevity, and the friends we've met through them continue to delight us. In early spring, we have fun eagerly checking each day to see if any green foliage is showing on the new plants we bought the previous year. In the summer, we wait excitedly for the first blossoms, whether they are from a newly purchased plant or from one of our own seedlings.

We confess that everything indicates that we have become badly addicted to daylilies; but considering the addictions and dependencies lurking around our culture these days, we could have become involved in much worse than daylilies, and we don't feel a bit guilty about inviting you to share our obsession.

Lewis and Nancy Hill
Greensboro, Vermont
August 1990

CHAPTER 1

Getting to Know the Amazing Daylily

WHEN WE STARTED TO GARDEN for the first time many years ago, one of the nursery catalogs we received described the daylily as "the perfect perennial." It went on to say that the plants were easy to grow, made an impressive showing, lived practically forever with almost no care, and were free of disease and insects. It sounded like the ideal plant for us, and we ordered several different varieties. They cost between nineteen cents and a dollar each.

We planted them in various places and were not disappointed, although the flowers themselves were not particularly interesting and did not rival our delphinium, lupine, or most other garden perennials in beauty. In the 1940s, the available daylilies had either yellow, dull orange, or rusty red blooms, and they all were about the same size and shape. Most of us growing them during those midcentury years did not dream of the possibilities lying latent in the common species and early hybrids.

Fortunately, a few visionary horticulturists suspected that hidden away in the daylily genes was the promise of blossoms of pink, white, bright red, purple, near-black, and possibly even blue. They envisioned ruffled edges, unusual color combinations, better fragrance, and a wide variety of flower shapes, sizes, and textures. Now, only a few decades later, their wildest dreams have been realized, and they confidently assure us that the best is yet to come.

The description of the daylily as the perfect flower is more accurate than ever before, as its ever-increasing popularity indicates. A prominent landscape contractor told us, "If I had to choose only one plant to put in a garden, it would be daylilies." It doesn't surprise us to learn that several leading perennial nurseries of the country have reported that the daylily is now their most popular plant.

Daylily Terminology

Although you can have a superior garden without knowing a single thing about plant terminology, it is helpful to have a passing knowledge of botanical terms when you are buying plants.

Hemerocallis is a *genus* in the plant family Liliaceae; it contains about two dozen species, and there are undoubtedly some species in remote parts of China not yet identified. A *species* is a group of plants that share most of the same characteristics as the rest of the genus but differ from other species in pronounced ways. Plant classification is not static, and it is not uncommon for botanists to change their minds about where a plant belongs. North American and European scientists do not always agree, either.

One of the species best known to North Americans is *Hemerocallis fulva*, the Tawny Daylily that escaped from pioneer gardens long ago. It blooms in mid-to-late summer and is often confused with the spotted orange Tiger Lily, which is also from the Orient but is one of the true lilies (*Lilium*). Daylily species are more fully described in Chapter 2.

Plant species often spawn numerous varieties — plants that are sufficiently different from the species to be noticeable, yet do not differ enough to be classified as separate species. Many such plants exist among daylily species, although their classification is not always agreed upon by the experts. For example, the common roadside 'Europa', the double 'Kwanso', 'Rosea', and other plants of the species *Hemerocallis fulva* are described by some authorities as varieties and by others, including our source, *Hortus Third*, as cultivars.

Ordinarily the term *cultivar*, a fairly new botanical term, is used to describe a plant that is officially named and registered. With daylilies this registration is done through the American Hemerocallis Society (AHS). A cultivar (also called a horticultural variety) is created either by an accident of nature or by breeders and is perpetuated under cultivation. Because the term "cultivar" is not yet in general use, you may hear the word "variety" commonly used in its place. The first letter of the name of a cultivar is capitalized, and it is common practice among daylily writers to capitalize the entire name of a cultivar. Thus 'Kwanso' might also be KWANSO in a daylily article. In scientific writing, however, only the first letter of a cultivar is capitalized and the name is enclosed in single quotes, such as, *Hemerocallis fulva* 'Kwanso', or the abbreviation "cv." is used before it, such as *H. fulva* cv. Kwanso.

Just What Is a Daylily?

Daylily lovers tend to become defensive when our favorite plant is misunderstood, as it often is. We don't like to have it confused with the Easter Lily, Tiger Lily, or the Regals and are likely to make a fuss when the name is spelled day lily, or daylilly. We point out that the plant does not grow from a bulb like a true lily (genus *Lilium*), nor from a corm, rhizome, or tuber. The roots are fibrous like those of most other herbaceous perennials and grow into clumps that can be easily split apart. Daylily roots are more fleshy than those of phlox, delphinium, and chrysanthemum but are not as woody as those of peonies.

The blooms of the daylily also differ from those of *Lilium*. Its buds form on a leafless stem, called a scape, that rises well above the leaves, unlike those of the true lily which bloom on the same stem as the foliage. Each blossom lasts only one day on most cultivars, a characteristic that provides its botanical name *Hemerocallis* (hem-ur-oh-KAL-is), given by Linnaeus in 1793, and meaning, in Greek, "beauty for a day." The flowers of most plants open in the morning, then fade and die in early evening. This seeming disadvantage is hardly noticed by casual observers, however, since a mature daylily plant produces so many buds that masses of flowers cover the clump every day for several weeks. This daily transformation actually can be a real advantage. Whenever a wind or a hard rainstorm injures all the blossoms in our fields, the damage shows for only that one day, and a fresh new crop of perfect blooms bursts forth the next morning. Flower arrangers are sometimes unhappy with the short life of their arrangements, however, and bemoan the fact that a carefully planned artistic creation may not last through a late-evening dinner party.

The foliage of the *Hemerocallis*, quite unlike that of the *Lilium*, grows in a clump of grasslike, sword-shaped leaves. The leaves of different kinds, though similar in appearance, range from very narrow to an inch or more in width, and their height may vary from only a few inches to over 2 feet.

A large daylily clump can be divided into many separate segments called fans. Each fan consists of roots and foliage, and after it is separated from the clump, it can be planted to start a new plant. When daylilies are sold, the plant usually consists of two or more fans, although when a new cultivar is in short supply, a nursery will often ship plants with only one.

One of the nice things about daylilies is that they grow well over so much of the world. There are kinds that flourish over nearly all the temperate zones, others that do well in subtropical areas, and still others in near-tropical conditions. In Florida and the Southwest, many kinds of daylilies flourish, even though most of the perennials grown in the rest of the United States and Canada do poorly there.

The extraordinary range of forms and colors in the genus *Hemerocallis* today provides plants to suit nearly everyone's taste and landscaping needs. One or another is at home everywhere, in a formal or informal flower bed, a wildflower planting, a color garden where all the flowers are the same color, a slope too difficult to mow, a roadside planting, around the foundation of a house or another building, or in a container breathing life into a city terrace.

In height, daylily flower scapes range from a Lilliputian few inches to a giant 6 feet, and the flower size may be as small as a large violet or up to 9 inches in diameter. The blooms run the gamut of shapes as well as sizes and may be lily-shaped, flat, rounding, double, triangular, or in a loose "spider" form. Some petals have silky smooth textures, others are rough or ruffled, and some have crinkled "piecrust" edgings.

The variety of colors covers nearly the entire spectrum in an artist's palette. Only pure black, pure white, and true blue are lacking, and breeders have not only come very close to achieving the first two, but they are certain that true blue will eventually appear among their experimental seedlings. Many blossoms contain vivid and unusual color combinations in the form of blotches, halos, and contrasting edgings.

Daylily foliage also varies widely in texture, size, and color, although most of us are not aware of foliage when the flowers are in bloom. Some of the miniatures have insignificant amounts of narrow, grasslike leaves, in contrast to the more vigorous kinds that produce massive clumps of foliage. The more energetic types are obviously the best choices if you need foundation plants around a house, where a green, shrublike mass is desirable even when the plant is not in bloom. Foliage color varies from a rich, dark green to blue-green, and a few varieties have variegated green-and-white leaves.

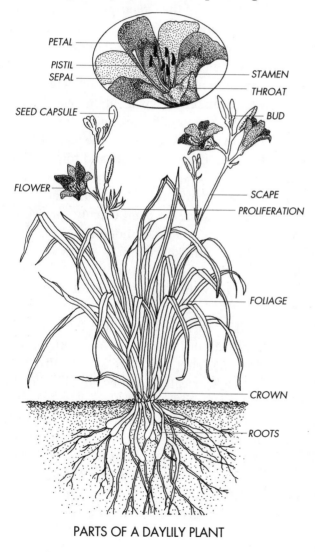

PARTS OF A DAYLILY PLANT

C H A P T E R 2

The Daylily:
From Past to Present Glory

"Consider the lilies of the field, how they grow; they toil not, neither do they spin, yet Solomon in all his glory was not arrayed like one of these."

— Matt. 6:28

ALTHOUGH THE "LILY" in the translation of this well-known quotation has been determined to be an anemone or another Palestinian wildflower, if daylilies had been growing in the Middle East at that time, Jesus could have aptly been pointing out their characteristics. Actually, the plant probably did not reach the Mediterranean until the sixteenth century. From the writings of early herbalists we know that both the Tawny Daylily *(Hemerocallis fulva)*, and the Lemon Daylily *(H. lilioasphodelus)*, were in Europe at that time and were probably brought there by traders.

As with printing, fireworks, and silk, the daylily had its origin in the East. All of the species now recognized were originally natives of Japan, Siberia, Korea, China, or Eurasia. The plants were valued through-out the Orient both for food and medicine as well as beauty, and the flowers appear often in Oriental art and legends.

Even though the immigrants to North America found a wealth of plant life when they arrived, there were no native species of *Hemerocallis*. The Tawny and Lemon Daylilies were among the first species to be brought, and their divisions were soon planted throughout the continent. The ease of their culture and the fact that they could be easily moved from place to place appealed to the hardworking pioneers, and a clump of daylilies, a lilac bush, and a peony plant were often the only ornamentals on a frontier homestead. The durability of these three plants, all transplanted originally from the old country, is still evident on long-abandoned farms in our area, where they still bravely bloom around an old cellar hole after a century or more of neglect. The vigorous Tawny Daylily, in fact, adapted so well to life in the new hemisphere that it became our familiar "roadside lily" and is now considered a common weed throughout much of eastern North America.

It is puzzling that although horticulturists in Europe worked energetically to develop better roses, lilacs, grapes, apples, and other plants, they neglected the daylily for centuries. It was not until the late 1800s and the first part of the twentieth century that interest became high. Plant collectors brought new daylilies from China, and breeders began to cross-pollinate various species and to create the multitude of hybrids that we enjoy today.

George Yeld, an English schoolteacher, was one of the first who saw the possibilities in *Hemerocallis* and set out to improve it. Apricot, his first known hybrid, was introduced in 1892. In the fifty-nine years that he continued his experimentation, he developed many cultivars. Some of these, including 'Tangerine' and 'Radiant', are still being grown in daylily gardens.

Amos Perry, a nurseryman in Enfield, England, continued Yeld's interest and developed and named over a hundred cultivars. Of the few still in existence today, the rugged 'Thelma Perry', 'Margaret Perry', and 'George Yeld' are most often seen.

Other early European hybridizers who contributed many fine new cultivars to the list were H. Christ of Germany, Victor Lemoine of France, Karl Sprenger and Willy Muller of Italy, and C. G. van Tuberman of Holland. Interest in developing new daylilies was high in England after World War II, when the noted breeders L. W. Brummitt, Lady Carew Pole, and H. J. Randall were active. When they stopped hybridizing, however, little went on in the daylily field among British horticulturists for many years. It was left to other European countries and North America to make the great strides that have subsequently taken place.

Among the pioneer North American daylily breeders was A. Herrington of New Jersey, whose Florham, registered in 1899, is thought to be the first cultivar that originated in North America. Others were Luther Burbank, who developed the well-known Calypso among others, and horticulturists Paul Cook, who developed 'Valiant', and Franklin Mead, who in 1924 originated 'Hyperion', which even now holds the unofficial record of being the best-known daylily of all time. Many other worthwhile cultivars were also introduced by Carl Betscher, Mrs. Thomas Nesmith, the Sass Brothers, and Ralph Wheeler.

Without a doubt, the giant of the daylily breeders in the first half of the twentieth century was Dr. Arlow Burdette Stout, better known as A. B. Stout, Director of Laboratories first, and later Curator of Education and Laboratories at the New York Botanical Garden. The history of the daylily would read quite differently without his contributions. As a young boy, he says in his autobiography, he noticed that his mother's Tawny Daylily produced no seed pods, and he was so curious to find out why, that he started a quest of more than thirty years. He eventually determined that it was because the Tawny Daylily was a triploid and usually sterile because of a condition known as irregular sporogenesis.

He began to hybridize in the late 1920s, and his scientific approach to plant development paved the way for many later breeders. He was the first to cross *H. fulva* 'Rosea' and other red-flowering daylilies with some of the existing yellow and orange daylilies, thus producing a large number of seedlings with a wide range of colors. The nearly 100 cultivars he selected and introduced from the hundreds of thousands of seedlings he raised include several still being grown: 'Mikado', 'Symphony', 'Theron', and 'Wau Bun'. Admirers still collect many of his early introductions, and some of his cultivars that have disappeared provided breeding material that led to many of today's beautiful specimens.

Stout was born in 1876, taught school for several years, and then attended the University of Wisconsin, where he majored in botany. In 1911, he joined the staff of the New York Botanical Garden, and it was there that he did most of his daylily research. He also worked with the New York State Experimental Station to develop 175 hardy seedless grape varieties; and he did extensive research on avocados, potatoes, apples, cherries, date palms, and many other flowers and vegetables.

Stout died in 1957 at the age of 81. Few people have devoted so much of their lives to the field of horticulture; the enormous number of papers that he wrote are still widely used by researchers. If you are interested in learning more of the history of early daylily development, Stout's famous book *Daylilies,* reprinted in 1986 by Sagapress, is necessary reading. The prestigious Stout Medal, the highest award for a daylily cultivar, is named in his honor.

Stout, in his book, gives credit to the many collectors who sent daylily plants and seeds to the New York Botanical Garden, particularly from Japan, China, and Manchuria. Dr. Albert Steward, a botany professor at the University of Nanking, was one such contributor, and his efforts greatly advanced the study of *Hemerocallis.*

Dr. Stout, Dr. Steward, and their contemporaries would no doubt be astonished at the incredible explosion of daylily cultivars in the past fifty years and especially at what is happening now. Thousands of horticulturists are at work trying to originate new ones. Some are backyard hobbyists, known in the trade as "pollen daubers," and others produce seedlings by the acre. Only a small percentage of these seedlings are named, registered, and introduced each year, and of those, only a few become well known. Some people introduce their plants in their own modest nurseries; others are lucky enough to have them offered by giant mail-order firms that grow hundreds of acres of plants. When you search through some of the many daylily nursery catalogs that are printed each year, you will become familiar with the names of such prolific and well-known modern originators as Apps, Barth, Childs, Claar, Durio, Elliot, Fay, Grovatt, Guidry, Hall, Harris, Harrison, Henry, Hudson, Jablonski, Joiner, Kennedy, King, Kirchhoff, Kraus, Lachman, MacMillan, Marsh, Marvin, Moldovan, Monette, Munson, Peck, Pierce, Rasmussen, Reckamp, Reilly, Seawright, Spalding, Wild, Williamson, and Yancey.

The Ancestors of the Modern Daylily

Although few of the wild species are now being sold by nurseries or cultivated in North American gardens, we list them here because they are of interest to daylily enthusiasts and hybridizers. If you want to raise wild species, a few nurseries still carry them, or you may be able to find them growing either along country roadsides where they have naturalized, or on abandoned homesteads where they were planted many years ago. Usually the landowners will be glad to give you permission to dig out a plant or two.

Thirteen or fourteen species of the genus *Hemerocallis* were recognized by Dr. Stout, and nearly a dozen have been discovered and identified since, many by Dr. Shiu-Ying Hu. The following list includes the most common species of *Hemerocallis* and some of the characteristics of each one that breeders have used to develop new cultivars. All species are hardy in the North unless otherwise noted, and the heights given refer to the scape (flower stalk) rather than to the foliage.

Hemerocallis altissima. As its Latin name implies, this is the tallest growing of the species and may reach more than 7 feet in height, although it is usually somewhat shorter. The flowers are light yellow, fragrant, of medium size, and bloom at night. *H. altissima* has been used by propagators to breed tall-growing daylilies suitable for the back of the border, or to make use of its night-blooming genes. Among the many cultivars that have been developed from *H. altissima* are the popular 'Autumn Minaret', with golden yellow flowers, and 'Challenger', a late bloomer with brick-red, 5-inch blooms.

H. aurantiaca. This orange daylily, from either China or Japan, grows about 3 feet tall and has 3-inch, burnt orange blooms in early summer. It is a rather coarse plant with evergreen foliage and is not generally hardy in the North. Hybridizers use some of its varieties — such as *major* with large red-orange blooms, and *littorea* with narrow petals and a rusty-red color — to develop late-blooming evergreens and semi-evergreens.

H. citrina. The nocturnal Citron Daylily also originated in China. It grows about 3 feet tall and in midsummer produces an abundance of lemon-yellow, fragrant flowers that open just before sunset. The plants are vigorous and very hardy, but its foliage has a tendency to die in early fall, making the plant unsightly from then on. It is not considered a good garden flower but has been widely used for breeding hardy, fragrant cultivars.

H. dumortieri. The Dumortieri or Early Daylily originated in Japan. It grows from 1 to 2 feet in height and has dark brown buds and pale orange, slightly fragrant flowers that are still seen blooming in many gardens in early spring. Their early-blooming habit, vigor, and hardiness made them popular in this country more than a century ago, and they are still extensively used for covering banks, as foundation plants around barns and sheds, and as borders for semiwild pathways. The roots are large and are sometimes used for eating in early spring, as are the fat, brown buds and flowers. The Dumortieri is often mistakenly called the "Lemon Lily," but it is more orange, more vigorous growing, and not nearly as fragrant. Hybridizers still use it to introduce hardiness, vigor, and heavy-blooming properties into their progeny.

H. forrestii. Forrest's Daylily, from southern China, grows from 1 to 2 feet tall and blooms early with clear yellow flowers. It has little going for it except its early blooming, however, and is much too tender for northern gardens.

H. fulva. The Tawny or Orange Daylily has spread widely throughout Asia, Europe, and North America. Its origin is uncertain but is thought to be Japan. The medium-large, sometimes double, orange-red flowers appear in midsummer. Unlike many other daylily species, *H. fulva* reproduces rapidly by spreading its underground stolons and can quickly cover a large area. This characteristic, plus the fact that it tolerates both full sun and more shade than most other daylilies, makes it ideal as a colorful ground cover in difficult places, as long as its rather weedy growth habit doesn't present a problem.

Of the two dozen or more daylilies in this species, 'Europa' is the best known. It was introduced to Europe during the Middle Ages and came to North America at an early date. It "escaped" long ago from cultivation on both continents, and in eastern North America it is commonly known as the "roadside lily" and, as we said earlier, is mistakenly called Tiger Lily.

'Kwanso' has double blossoms and, occasionally, variegated foliage. These characteristics have made it useful in developing hybrids. Like 'Europa', the roots of 'Kwanso' are stoloniferous and have a similar ability to produce new plants rapidly. *H. fulva* 'Rosea' has been extensively used for breeding pink and red daylilies.

H. lilioasphodelus (formerly *H. flava*). The Lemon Lily or Lemon Daylily originated in eastern Asia, probably China. It grows to 3 feet and has very early, light yellow, medium-sized, fragrant blooms. It was popular with the early settlers in North America and, like *H. dumortieri*, is still grown in old-fashioned gardens. It is not particularly vigorous and tends to grow into a rather sprawling plant instead of a neat clump, but it can survive and flower for decades even if completely neglected. Although it is not a heavy bloomer, the clear, cool yellow blossoms are easy to spot even in a field of weeds.

The Lemon Daylily is diurnal, but it is an extended bloomer, meaning that its flowers last well into the night and sometimes even into the second day. Needless to say, it is the ancestor of many of our modern cultivars and is used particularly to develop early-blooming, fragrant, extended-blooming hybrids.

H. middendorffii. The Middendorff or Amur Daylily grows wild in Siberia, China, Korea, and Japan. The scape grows from 1 to 2 feet tall and is often confused with *H. dumortieri,* which it resembles in vigor and color of bloom. More than once when we wanted to get rid of a planting of either of these species, we had difficulty because of their tenaciousness, and it was years before we dared to replant the area to more refined cultivars.

Once widely grown for their early, pale orange, 3-inch blooms, Middendorff, like Dumortieri, is seldom found in nurseries today; but we often see them growing in older gardens. The cultivar Major blooms more heavily than the rest of the species but otherwise is very similar. In the Orient, the buds of Middendorff are a popular food.

H. minor. The Grass-leaf Daylily is native from Japan to Siberia. A dwarf plant with yellow blooms, it grows from 1 to 2 feet in height. The slim, slender roots are not as fleshy as those of most species, and its long, narrow, grasslike leaves become dormant early in the fall. The small, fragrant flowers appear early in the season, soon after those of the Lemon Daylily, and they are slightly fragrant. This species is seldom sold by nurseries or grown in home gardens, but it has been widely used as a parent for breeding dwarf, small-flowered cultivars.

H. multiflora. The Mayflower or Many-flowered Daylily from China grows about 3 feet tall and has small, orange flowers. It blooms in late summer and fall, not heavily at any one time, although it flowers over a long season. It is not often grown as a garden plant, but it has been used for breeding some popular miniature cultivars.

H. nana. This dwarf daylily from China grows to about 18 inches and has small, fragrant, orange flowers; the petals are brownish on the back. The flowers are approximately 3 inches in diameter and usually only one is borne on each scape. The leaves are usually longer than the scapes, and the plants are less vigorous than either *H. lilioasphodelus* or *H. dumortieri.* It has been somewhat used in developing shorter cultivars.

H. thunbergii. The Thunberg Daylily is a nocturnal bloomer from Japan and grows 3 or more feet in height. The 3-inch, clear yellow, fragrant flowers open at night in mid-to-late summer. The plants are vigorous and were quite widely grown in North American and European gardens a century ago. Thunberg blooms resemble the Lemon Daylily in appearance but come much later in the season. They have been used for breeding fragrant, yellow bloomers.

CHAPTER 3

Speaking Daylily Language

SOON AFTER WE BECAME seriously interested in daylilies as a specialty, we joined a garden tour in eastern Massachusetts which was sponsored by the New England Region of the American Hemerocallis Society. As we listened in on the conversations of the people walking up and down the rows around us, it didn't take us long to realize that there was a lot more to daylily growing and breeding than we had first realized. While we were busy jotting down names of the different kinds that appealed to us, the more experienced members chatted about textures, tetraploids, semi-evergreens, and diamond dusting, and pointed out watermarks, halos, and polychromes. They tossed around cultivar names as if they were best friends: 'Florence Byrd', 'Lemoine Bechtold', and 'Grandfather Time'. The flowers obviously meant much more to these discerning folks than just the spectacular masses of blooms we were seeing.

Although we still love daylilies in large, colorful fields and hope never to become too discriminating to enjoy, in Wordsworth's words, the "meanest flower that blows," we did our homework and were soon able to look with more understanding at daylilies and to better appreciate their finer points.

Daylily terminology has developed not for snob appeal, but because new terms became necessary as hybridizers originated new cultivars that did not fit the current language. To clear up the confusion between the old and new terms, the American Hemerocallis Society has developed an effective system to classify daylily plants, their flowers, and their foliage.

A knowledge of the different parts of the plant is essential to an understanding of daylily terms. Like most plants, they consist of the *roots, foliage,* and *crown* (where the roots and foliage meet at ground level or slightly below). Daylily buds are formed on *scapes* — leafless stalks that stand above their grasslike foliage.

The bloom of a single daylily flower consists of six segments — three *petals* and three *sepals* (see illustration, page 6). When these are all the same color they are referred to as a *self*. The *throat*, where the flower meets the stem, is often a different color from the rest of the bloom. Protruding from the throat are eight *stamens*, the male parts of the flower, which produce the *pollen*. Daylily pollen is usually brown but may also be a reddish or yellow color, and it may or may not be fertile. In the center of the stamens and protruding out beyond them is the single *pistil*, the female organ that receives the pollen.

Daylily flowers can be described in many ways according to their form, color, and color pattern as well as their size, substance, shape, and texture.

Flaring. Unusually open with rather flat petals and sepals.

Trumpet. Traditional lily shape.

Recurved. As with a flaring shape, petals and sepals stretch back from throat, but in this case, tips of both curve back toward the scape.

Circular. Because of the shape of the petals and sepals, and the way they overlap, flower appears quite round.

Flower Forms

The flower forms of *hems*, as daylilies are sometimes called, can be defined as circular, double, flaring, flat, oval, pinwheel, recurved, spider, star, triangular, or trumpet. Most descriptions speak for themselves, although some need explanation. A *flaring* shape, for example, is one that is unusually open and rather flat; *recurved* means that the

Double. In addition to the usual three petals and three sepals, extra flower segments result in blooms that may vary from slightly double to peonylike.

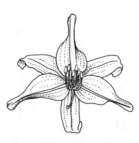

Star. Long, pointed petals and sepals, with spaces between, resembling a three- or six-pointed star.

Spider. Petals and sepals are quite narrow throughout their length, with little or no taper.

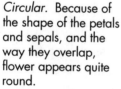

tips of both the petals and sepals are curved back toward the stem; *trumpet* is the traditional lily shape, and *star* indicates that, with a little imagination, the flower resembles a star. *Informal* is a classification that is sometimes used for flowers that do not fit any of the other categories.

Double daylilies vary from the simple *hose-in-hose*, a single flower within a single flower, to those that are as double as peonies. Some daylily cultivars produce blooms that are always double, and many that are not considered double occasionally produce both double and single blooms on the same plant, often at the same time.

Color Patterns

The colors of daylily flowers range from single shades to complex blendings and patterns. Most can be classified in one of the following categories:

Self — This term indicates that the flower segments (petals and sepals) are the same single color or shade, but the throat may be a different color. 'Green Flutter' has a greenish-yellow self, for example.

Blend — When the flower segments are a blending of two colors, such as yellow and pink, the flower is said to be a blend.

Polychrome — A flower that has an intermingling of many colors, such as melon, pink, lavender, and yellow is said to be a polychrome.

Bitone — The petals and sepals of a bitone daylily are in the same color range but differ in shade or intensity, with the petals a darker shade than the sepals. For example, the petals may be a dark rose pink and the sepals a lighter, pale pink. A *reverse bitone* has sepals that are a darker shade than the petals.

Bicolor — A *bicolor* daylily has petals and sepals of totally different colors, such as red

Self. Petals and sepals are the same color.

Bitone. Both petals and sepals are of a distinctly different shade or intensity of the same color, with sepals being lighter.

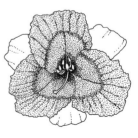

Blend. Petals and sepals are a blend of two colors, such as yellow and pink. In a polychrome, petals and sepals are a blend of several colors, such as melon, pink, lavender, and yellow.

Bicolor. Petals and sepals are of totally different colors; the sepals are the lighter shade.

Band. A different or darker colored band on the petals only at the point where the flower segments join the throat.

Eyezone. A different or darker colored band on both petals and sepals at the point where the flower segments join the throat.

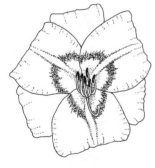

Halo. A very faint, or only slightly visible, band of a different or darker color.

Watermark. A wide stripe of a very light shade where the color of the petals and sepals joins the throat; gives the effect of a watermark.

and yellow. The sepals are lighter in shade or in color value. In a *reverse bicolor*, the sepals are a darker or stronger color and the petals are lighter.

Bands, Eyezones, Halo,* and *Watermarks — A distinguishing pattern on many daylilies is the band of a different color or darker shade of the same color at the juncture of the segments and the throat. This pattern is termed *eye* or *eyezone* if the differing or darker color is present on both petals and sepals. It is called a *band* if it occurs only on the petals. If the band of differing or darker color is faint or only slightly visible, it is called a *halo*. A band-type marking found in many new cultivars is a *watermark*, a wide stripe of a very light shade where the segment color meets the throat, giving a faint, barely visible watermark effect to the flower.

In addition to these categories, you may notice daylilies with other colorations. Some have a midrib of a different shade running up each petal, and others, a contrasting color on the tip or the edging of each petal. Sometimes you'll also find petals dotted with a different color, or entire throats of colors that are different from that of the segments. The stamens may be red, black, or lavender as well as the more common yellow or brown shades.

The daylily segments of certain cultivars may also be *diamond dusted*, a genetic characteristic that causes them to sparkle in the sunlight as if they were covered with millions of tiny sequins. This exotic dusting may be either silvery or golden.

Other Flower Features

In addition to form and color, there are other flower features you are likely to find in catalog descriptions:

The *substance* of a flower is the thickness of the tissue structure of its petals and sepals. Substance varies greatly from thin and very fragile to heavy and rugged, as in many tetraploids. Flowers with light substance tend to break easily in the wind and when they are picked or handled in an arrangement.

Texture refers to smoothness or roughness of the flower segments. Because smooth textures reflect the light better, they create a more vivid color.

The *size* of a flower varies from miniature blossoms, which are smaller than 3 inches in diameter, to *large* blossoms, over 4½ inches. Those that range from 3 to 4½ inches are considered to be *small flowered*.

The *height* of a plant refers to the height of the flower scape rather than its foliage. The scapes are classified as low (6 inches to 2 feet), *medium* (2 to 3 feet), and *tall* (over 3 feet). *Dwarf* refers to any plant with scapes less than 1 foot tall. Dwarfs may or may not have miniature flowers. Most people feel that the height of the scape should be somewhat in proportion to flower size for best appearance. Either large flowers on very short scapes or tiny flowers on 3-foot scapes may seem unbalanced.

The *branching habit* of a daylily refers to the way that the buds form on their scapes. The various habits are classified as *low*

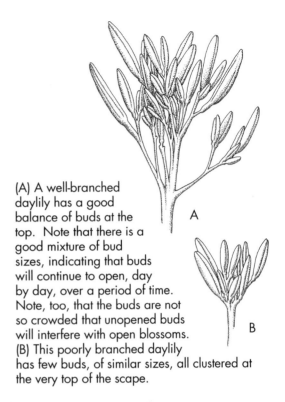

(A) A well-branched daylily has a good balance of buds at the top. Note that there is a good mixture of bud sizes, indicating that buds will continue to open, day by day, over a period of time. Note, too, that the buds are not so crowded that unopened buds will interfere with open blossoms. (B) This poorly branched daylily has few buds, of similar sizes, all clustered at the very top of the scape.

branched, when buds form near the base of the scape; *well branched*, when there is a good balance of buds on the scape; and *top branched*, when they form at the very top of the scape, well above the foliage, somewhat like an amaryllis.

Bud count refers to the number of buds on each scape. The number varies from less than ten to over fifty. Most older cultivars form all their buds before any of them open, and the buds continue to open at various times until none are left. If the bud count is "heavy," blooms will probably cover the plant nearly every day during the flowering season. Many of the newer cultivars are bred to continue to produce new buds during the blooming season. Others rest for a while after blooming and then rebloom a few weeks later.

Blooming Habits and Blooming Time

The *blooming habit* of a daylily is differentiated from its *blooming time*. "Habit" refers to the time of day the flowers open and how long the blooms last; "time" refers to the season in which it blooms.

Most cultivars are *diurnal,* which means that they open in the morning and close at night. Temperatures affect the timing; for example, in cool regions the flowers tend to open later in the morning and remain open longer in the evening. If the preceding night has been unusually chilly, the blooms of some cultivars may not fully open at all the next day, especially if there have been two cold nights in a row. This habit has been disconcerting to us and our daylily custom-

ers when occasionally our entire fields are filled with half-open, sickly appearing flowers on an August day! Fortunately it happens only once or twice each summer, but after freezing weather begins in September, our nights are often too cold for the flowers to bloom their best the following day.

Nocturnal bloomers open sometime during the early evening or night and usually close between late morning and early afternoon. Some cultivars that are nocturnal in warm climates do not always bloom at night in the cooler regions but behave like diurnals instead.

Both diurnal and nocturnal bloomers may also be *extended bloomers,* meaning that they stay open for sixteen hours or more. The diurnals may open in early morning and last until midnight, and nocturnals open sometime after 4 P.M. and stay open until into the next day. Certain new cultivars bloom for even longer periods. The nocturnal 'Pat Mercer', for example, does not produce especially beautiful flowers in most people's

KEY:

Height
T = Tall
M = Medium
S = Short

Bloom Times
1 = Extra early
2 = Early
3 = Midseason
4 = Late
5 = Extra late

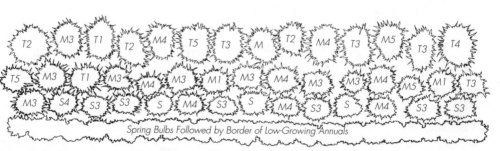

Spring Bulbs Followed by Border of Low-Growing Annuals

A mass planting of daylilies can provide color over a surprisingly long period if you choose cultivars of many different blooming times. This border is about eight to ten feet wide and thirty-five feet long; it could be repeated for a longer border. Northern summer vacation gardeners should omit the spring bulbs and the extra-late cultivars and substitute midseason cultivars that will bloom during vacation time.

estimation, but it has a particularly interesting blooming habit. It opens in the evening and displays its bright red flowers and green throat throughout the next day. The following day it stays open, but the flower becomes more orange and the throat changes to white.

The blooming season of daylilies varies considerably. The earliest ones may bloom as early as March in the South, or as late as the end of June in the North (Zones 3 and 4). For this reason, catalogs list blooming times as EE (extra early); E (early); EM (early midseason); M (midseason, which can be interpreted as May in the South, but as late July and August in the North); LM (late midseason); L (late); and VL (very late). Each designation must, of course, be interpreted to fit the climatic zone where the plants will be grown. Most daylily buds can tolerate several moderate frosts and still blossom, but the blooms, as we have mentioned, are not likely to be as attractive as those unscathed by cold temperatures.

In attempting to classify the blooming times of the different daylilies in our area, we have been frustrated by the fact that the same cultivars may behave differently in different years. 'Smoky Joe' bloomed in early midseason one year, for example, and in mid-September the next. After several years of observing 'Susan Elizabeth', one of our favorite giant yellows, we still are not sure whether it should be designated as

"early" or "midseason." The likely reason for this behavior is the crazy New England climate; in regions with more predictable weather patterns, the blooming times of daylilies are likely to be more consistent.

The amount of sunlight a plant gets and the time of day it receives it affects its blooming time. The 'Green Ice' daylilies on the northwest side of our house, which get a minimum of morning sun, bloom nearly two weeks later than those on the southeast side, where they bask in sunlight for most of the day. Plants that get a full day's sun in spring may get only a half day in late August if they are planted next to a southern wall, hedge, solid fence, or building, and this can delay their blooming time, too. Late afternoon shade can be beneficial for certain plants, however, even if it delays flowering. We have noticed that the blossoms of many of our red cultivars and some of the pinks have a much brighter color when they

The front of this house faces southwest. Daylily beds on the northwest side, which gets little morning sun, bloom as much as two weeks later than beds on the southeast and southwest sides, where they bask in sunlight for more of the day.

are growing where a tall arborvitae hedge shades them from the hot afternoon sun.

Length of the Blooming Period

The length of time that a mature daylily clump stays in bloom varies, and it depends a great deal on the species or cultivar. Most bloom from two to four weeks, but certain cultivars have the unique ability to produce buds over a long season. These *bud builders*, as they are called, are a desirable addition to a garden, since some produce blooms from late spring throughout the summer. The popular, dwarf 'Stella de Oro' is one of the best-known bud builders.

Other daylilies from which you glean more than the normal number of blooms are the *rebloomers*, which usually blossom for a few weeks, take a vacation, and then bloom again. In places where the first frosts may come in early September, though, few are able to produce enough second blooms to make them worth planting for that purpose.

In our garden we've noticed that we probably do not appreciate the late-blooming daylilies as much as we should. Our short growing season means that a lot of blooms are crowded into a few short weeks. We are always eager to see the first blossoms of the season, even though some may not be as nice as those that follow, and we treasure the great masses of flowers that dominate the gardens in midseason. But it is easy to nearly ignore the ones that flower especially late. Our reaction is, no doubt, caused by the fact that in northern gardens the cold nights of early autumn make many of the late bloomers look rather washed out, but also by autumn, we seem to be ready to enjoy the chrysanthemums, gloriosa daisies, asters, and anemones in their seasons. Blasphemy, for avid daylily lovers to even think such thoughts!

Foliage Types and Hardiness

Daylily catalogs usually state whether a daylily's foliage is *dormant* (Dor), *evergreen* (Ev), or *semi-evergreen* (Semi-ev), terms that, we all like to think, also indicate a plant's hardiness, although this isn't always true.

Dormants are considered to be the most hardy. Their foliage, like that of most other northern perennials, turns brown in late autumn and dies over the winter. The plants stay dormant until spring, which makes them ideal for northern gardens. Through snow, ice, winds, and cold temperatures during the winter, the dormant roots lie protected under the earth until warm spring rains signal that it's time to awake and send up sprouts. Most dormants also do well in warmer regions of the country, but some that were developed in the North do not grow well where there is little or no winter season. Unfortunately, there has not yet been enough research done on which plants are best suited for the far South or the far North. Growers must do their own experimenting or rely on neighboring gardeners for information.

Evergreens are the least hardy. Their foliage remains green all winter in the South, but in the North it is likely to turn brown. Because the plants are sensitive to periods of alternate freezing and thawing, they should be mulched where such conditions are likely, even though winter temperatures may not become extremely cold. A mulch also protects them from damage that might be caused if growth were to start too early in the spring. Fortunately, many of the evergreens are hardy enough to grow with a little protection even in Canada, and it is always tempting for Northerners to try them. Because so much modern hybridizing takes place in the South, there is a wider variety of brilliant colors and flower types among evergreens than among dormants.

Semi-evergreens vary considerably in hardiness. Although some skeptics have expressed the opinion that the term "semi-evergreen" was devised to make northern gardeners think the plant would grow in the North, and fool southern gardeners into believing that it would grow for them, too, this is not the case. "Semis" often result when hybridizers cross evergreens with dormants in an effort to combine the hardiness of dormants with the superior colors of evergreens.

In general the semis do well in the South, but not all succeed in the coldest areas of the North. In the South the tops of their foliage turn brown or yellow in the winter, and the lower parts stay green. In the North the foliage dies after cold weather develops, and the plant stays dormant for the rest of the winter.

Although most gardeners find the general classifications quite sufficient, daylily buffs add three more foliage types to the list. Of the six groups they use, the most hardy are the hard dormants, followed by the dormants, semidormants, semi-evergreens, evergreens, and soft evergreens.

Hard dormants become dormant very early in the autumn and stay dormant until late in the spring.

Semidormants become dormant later in the autumn, after a period of cold weather. They begin to grow again after a few warm days in the spring. Only the top foliage appears dead, however, and green sprouts often remain buried in the crown where winters are not too severe.

Soft evergreens are the least hardy of all daylilies and are suitable only for areas that experience almost completely frost-free winters.

These terms are meant to define as clearly as possible which daylilies will grow in which climatic conditions. The problem with taking the foliage classifications as gospel truth is that some evergreens are hardy in the North, and a few dormants are not. Likewise many dormants do well in southern zones, although some will not. So, although the various terms are helpful in choosing plants, they are not foolproof indications of hardiness. Unfortunately, most of the newest and most expensive cultivars have not yet stood the test of time and been thoroughly tested for cold or heat resistance before they are offered to the public.

In general, northern growers should use caution when buying evergreen daylilies from the most southern states and from

California and should also be wary of buying from catalogs that don't state whether the plants are dormant or evergreen. The most reliable way to obtain new plants that are suitable for your region is to buy those that have been raised at a nearby nursery. If you are like most of us, however, you will occasionally want to try some of the exciting new cultivars from another region and do your own experimentation.

Tetraploids and Diploids

Two words that often appear in daylily literature are *tetraploid* and *diploid*, which classify different types of daylilies according to their chromosome count. Like other plants, daylilies have in each of their cells (except those of the pollen and egg cells) a basic number of chromosomes. These contain the genes that carry the plant's genetic characteristics. Most daylilies are diploid, which means that they have two identical sets of eleven chromosomes (twenty-two total) in each cell. Polyploids are plants with more than two sets—a triploid has three sets, and a tetraploid has four, double the usual number (forty-four total).

When you look at a daylily, there's no way of telling for sure whether it is a diploid or a tetraploid, but as a general rule the tetraploids have flower substance that is heavier and pollen grains that are larger. "Tets," as they are called, also tend to have more vigor, foliage that is more dense, and flowers that are larger, more numerous, and of brighter colors.

The "miracle" of tetraploid conversion began in 1937, when it was discovered that the chemical colchicine, derived from the autumn crocus, could be used to increase the number of chromosomes in iris and other plants. Although the number sometimes increases naturally, or is increased by scientists using extreme heat or cold, or by the uniting of unreduced cells in sexual reproduction, the discovery of the amazing power of colchicine to create a whole new group of plants produced a great deal of excitement.

Daylily breeders rushed to experiment with the new conversion process. Colchicine, however, is an extremely poisonous alkaloid, highly toxic to both people and plants, and thus had to be handled very carefully. Furthermore, the first amateur daylily breeders using colchicine were not very successful, and many felt satisfied if they achieved a conversion rate as large as 5 percent. Because of these factors, many plant breeders decided that it was more feasible for them to hybridize the cultivars that had already been converted to tetraploids and leave the painstaking conversion process to experts. The situation might be compared to that created by home computers when they were in their infancy. The first owners felt compelled to take courses on how to write their own programs, but most soon learned that it was far more practical to take advantage of the professionally written software that quickly became available.

When the first tets of note — the

Crestwood Series — were introduced in 1961 by Orville Fay, a well-known breeder, and Robert Griesbach, a geneticist, they created a sensation in the daylily world. Their cultivars, 'Crestwood Ann' and 'Crestwood Evening', sold for $100 each, an enormous price at that time. Today some of the older tets sell for as little as $3, although new originations may be priced at several hundred dollars.

New tets are usually created by treating the sprouting seeds or young seedlings with colchicine, but the chemical is also sometimes used to convert the plants of existing cultivars. Thus, in some catalogs you may find the tetraploid form of a certain daylily cultivar listed along with the diploid form. Comparing the blooms of the two is always interesting. Sometimes the difference is very noticeable, but occasionally it is difficult to tell them apart.

Some growers fear that there may be weaknesses in tetraploid daylilies that are likely to show up in future years, although there has been little evidence of any such problems to date. There is evidence, too, that a few of the so-called tetraploids that have been introduced are not tets at all. Occasionally, plants have never been thoroughly checked to see if the colchicine treatment actually worked. The pollen of tets, as we've said, is usually much larger than that of the diploids, and this factor has often been used to determine the conversion, rather than the accurate but more difficult method of actually counting the chromosomes under a microscope.

Are tets better than diploids in every way? As with many new ideas, after the enthusiasm came the doubts. In the late 1930s, breeders had great success creating tetraploid bearded iris, and a new breed of giant iris resulted. Although breeders expected the same extraordinary results with daylilies, their expectations have been only partially realized, and many of the newer diploids rival them in every way. We now have a wide choice of sensational daylilies in both diploid and tetraploid form. It is fascinating to know about chromosome counts, but most of us don't need to worry much about the differences between the two. Like apples and peaches, rather than comparing, we enjoy them both. When we fall in love with a certain daylily that has characteristics we like, we buy it with little concern over whether it is diploid or tetraploid. Beauty, vigor, blooming habits, and other such qualities are what count when we are choosing a new daylily for our garden.

Miniatures

Although the large-flowering daylilies have always won the most popularity contests, those with miniature blooms have recently become sought after by many connoisseurs. "Miniature" refers to daylilies that are classed according to their blooms of less than 3 inches in diameter. They can be found on tall-growing scapes, but the term is now likely to refer to cultivars that produce small blooms and grow only 12 to 18 inches tall.

Modern breeders have had excellent

results in creating hybrid cultivars that not only meet these requirements of bloom size and scape height, but also come in a wide range of colors. Many have ruffled petals and some have centers or edgings of contrasting colors. Some cultivars, such as 'Stella de Oro', bloom over a long season. Miniatures are ideal for certain locations such as small gardens, edgings in larger plantings, or for use in pots, planters, or rock gardens.

Spiders

Daddy longlegs come to mind when we look at spider daylilies. Long, spidery petals and sepals extend from their throats, forming blossoms that are sometimes more than 9 inches in diameter. Even though they are showy, they are not everyone's favorite, and you are likely either to be very fond of them or not like them at all.

There is considerable dispute among growers about what constitutes a true spider. The American Hemerocallis Society has concluded that a bona fide specimen must have a 5 to 1 ratio between the length of its petals and their width, but some feel that this ratio is too high, and that many of the blooms presently described as "spider-like" should be classified as true spiders.

Lemoine Bechtold is regarded as the pioneer breeder of spider daylilies. Some of the spiders and near-spiders he introduced in the early 1950s were 'Garden Portrait', 'Kindly Light', 'Nian', 'Shirley Wild', and 'Winegar'. Although all of these are still popular, since its introduction the large, golden yellow 'Kindly Light' has endured as the spider to which all others are compared.

After the first excitement, interest in the spiders seemed to wane, and except for a few dedicated individuals who continued to work with them, the breeding of new cultivars nearly ceased in the decades directly following World War II. In recent years, however, renewed interest has spurred experimenters to once again introduce new spider and spider-type cultivars. Although not many make the "100 most popular," they have a long list of admirers, and some gardeners grow spiders exclusively. Their increasing popularity is confirmed by the amount of space devoted to them in each issue of the *Daylily Journal*. Spiders fit well into a flower border and almost anywhere else daylilies are used, but they appear most at home in informal and semiwild gardens, where their natural look is particularly appealing.

Fragrant Daylilies

Visitors love to sniff the daylily blooms in our gardens and often leave with pollen-tipped noses. Many of the wild species are fragrant, including the well-known Lemon Daylily (*H. lilioasphodelus*), which has one of the best scents. The cultivar 'Hyperion', another old favorite, is also valued for its delightful aroma as well as its large, clear yellow blooms. These and others have long been used in the breeding of fragrant cultivars, but fragrance remains a somewhat elusive factor in hybridization. It often fails to appear in a new seedling even if both its parents are fragrant; a more dominant gene apparently takes over in the mating process. As a result, the list of good daylilies with noticeable fragrance remains disappointingly small.

A good way to detect fragrance without sniffing every bloom is to watch the bees. When they favor a flower, it is likely to be one with a scent. If you expect daylilies to have the overpowering aroma of a regal lily or daphne, however, you'll probably be disappointed. Daylily fragrance tends to be light, and it varies at different times of the day. It is likely to be strongest in early evening and may change from day to day, depending on temperature and humidity. The aroma of a large clump of flowers may be particularly noticeable when the air is quiet on a warm evening or when they are arranged in a bouquet. See Chapter 15 for popular fragrant varieties.

The Classics

In every type of daylily grouping, classic names pop up again and again in daylily conversations and writings. Like classics of literature that sometimes outlive other works by dint of reputation alone, these "classic" cultivars are not always superior in every way to all the older kinds, and some may fail badly when compared with recently introduced hybrids. Therefore, we feel that no one should rely too much on this list. Not only do daylily classics change

over the years, but opinions differ in various sections of North America. With the thousands of cultivars and millions of daylily growers, it would be miraculous to get unanimous agreement on classics or anything else having to do with gardening. Most are, nevertheless, fine cultivars and have become so well known that many growers regard them as standards to which other daylilies in their groupings are compared.

'American Revolution' is a star candidate for a classic among the dark, deep reds, but there are many others. (We particularly like 'New England Night', as well.) 'American Revolution' was developed in 1972 by the famous Wilds of Sarcoxie, Missouri. It has dormant foliage and 5-inch, velvety black-red blossoms on 28-inch scapes.

'Dance Ballerina Dance' has become a classic among daylilies with large, ruffled blooms. Developed in 1976 by Virginia Peck, its 6-inch blossoms are an apricot-pink shade and are so heavily ruffled that they sometimes do not open completely. This dormant tetraploid grows about 2 feet tall. Since its introduction, it has been extensively used for hybridizing and has spawned a host of other ruffled daylilies.

'Ed Murray' is considered by many as the standard for judging bright reds and has made the list of the "100 most popular" for years. Two decades have not diminished this diploid's fame, since Edward Grovatt developed it in 1970. Its round and slightly ruffled petals are faintly white edged. It is also available in a converted tetraploid form that has been successfully for breeding.

'Hyperion', originated in 1924 by Franklin B. Mead, is said to have resulted from a cross between 'Sir Michael Foster' and 'Florham'. Introduced in 1925, it has remained the standard yellow daylily for decades and is still widely grown, even though many nurseries consider it too passé to be carried. It is very vigorous and produces a large number of 5- to 6-inch canary yellow blooms on sturdy stems about 3 feet tall. The plant blooms for several weeks in midsummer, and each blossom stays open well into the evening. 'Hyperion' is considered one of the best choices for mass plantings.

'Joan Senior', an evergreen, is in the running for a classic near-white. Although it is a diploid, a converted tetraploid form of it is also available. The slightly ruffled, 6-inch blooms on 2-foot scapes appear in early summer. It was introduced by Kenneth Durio in 1977.

'Kindly Light' has remained the classic spider since its origination in 1950 by Lemoine Bechtold. Its huge, 8-inch flowers and loose, twisted petals with ruffled edges made it a hit at once, even though its form was quite unlike that of the usual daylily. Its enduring popularity is evidenced by the fact that it won the Harris Olson spider award thirty-nine years later, in 1989.

'Stella de Oro' is a classic miniature that is nearly always mentioned when exceedingly long bloomers are being discussed. A seedling raised by Walter Jablonski, it was introduced in 1975. Its slightly ruffled, golden yellow blooms with tiny green throats are less than 3 inches in diameter, and are borne abundantly on 12- to 18-inch scapes. It is one of the earliest daylilies to bloom and continues to produce new buds and rebloom throughout the summer and into the fall. The plant is a very hardy dormant. Because of its many attributes, it has been widely used for breeding purposes, and some of its offspring, 'Super Stella' and 'Stella Junior', were also introduced by Jablonski.

C H A P T E R 4

The Versatile Daylily — At Home Almost Everywhere

A CLUMP OF DAYLILIES in full flower will turn the head of the most apathetic viewer, but don't be misled by the outward beauty of a daylily when you see it decorating a fine formal border or gracefully blowing in the wind. Like Cleopatra or Joan of Arc, underneath their lovely exteriors most are tough characters and are able to withstand many difficulties. They will grow in soils that you'd think no plant could love, survive drought and wind and rainstorm, and compete successfully with other vegetation for their space. The combination of these stubborn characteristics and their attractive clumplike foliage and beautiful blossoms makes them ideal perennials for planting almost anywhere in the landscape. They do well not only in a well-tended border, but also around a foundation, on a slope for stopping erosion, or edging a winding gar-

den path. At the risk of sounding like a commercial, the truth is that no matter what location you have for planting, there is likely to be some type of daylily to fill your need.

In general, the plants do best when they are growing in full sunlight, but most will thrive if they get only a half day of full sun and a half day of skylight. They do just fine when grown on the southwest or northeast side of a hedge, building, or wall. The old 'Tawny' and its cultivars, 'Europa', 'Rosea', and 'Kwanso', grow and bloom even in moderate shade.

Like daffodils, large plantings of daylilies look best if groupings of the same colors are together. Expert landscapers know that drifts of single colors look best, the size of each color mass to be determined by the size of the bed. The larger the entire planting, the larger each drift should be.

Vigorous daylilies that have proven reliable for slopes, foundations, edgings, mass plantings, and commercial landscaping are:

Bell Tel
Diamond Anniversary
Dumortieri
Europa (particularly for shade)
Formal Affair
Green Ice
Hyperion
Imperator
Sandalwood
Winning Ways

Using Daylilies in the Mixed Flower Border

The term "border" covers many kinds of gardens, including those that actually border a lawn, wall, hedge, or fence, as well as "island" beds that are surrounded by lawn. They can be formal and balanced, precisely designed with straight-edged lines, or informal with curved, irregular shapes.

Daylilies are impressive in any kind of border whenever they are in bloom, but if you want color throughout the spring, summer, and autumn, it will be necessary to combine them with other perennials and with annuals. The grasslike leaves of the various kinds of daylilies are so similar that when the plants are not in bloom, some people feel that the texture of the garden looks rather monotonous. A mixture of different perennials with diverse foliage adds interest to the garden in all seasons.

Most gardeners use spring bulbs to start the floral display. Almost any kind of bulb that grows well in your region will be satisfying. The long-lived crocuses, daffodils, grape hyacinths, and snowdrops do not need to be replaced as frequently as tulips and hyacinths, but the blooms of all spring flowers are heartwarming after a dreary winter.

After the spring bulbs have finished blooming, a selection of early-flowering perennials can be used to complement the earliest-blooming daylilies such as 'Bitsy', 'Butterscotch Ruffles', 'Citation', 'Dumortieri', 'Enchanted Elf', 'Gem', Lemon Daylily, 'Lilac Greetings', 'May Splash', 'Pony Ride', 'Sooner Gold', 'Stella de Oro', 'Susie Wong', and 'Thumbelina'. For this purpose in our border we like bleedingheart, columbine, *Doronicum*, *Iberis*, primrose, *Pulmonaria*, and *Trollius*. A bit later, in early summer, *Anthemis*, coralbells, delphinium, iris, lilies, lupine, Oriental poppy, peony, Siberian iris, and sweet William are good complementary plants.

About the time the primary groups of daylilies begin to flower, many other popular perennials also bloom, including *Achillea*, *Anthemis*, *Astilbe*, bee balm, *Coreopsis*, crane's-bill, foxglove, *Gaillardia*, globe thistle, *Heliopsis*, hosta, *Liatris*, lilies, monkshood, phlox, *Rudbeckia*, sage, sedum, Shasta daisy, and veronica.

Many of these perennials go well with daylilies. We particularly like to use clumps

▲ From center front, clockwise: *Hemerocallis* 'Green Flutter', *Filipendula rubra, Lythrum virgatum* 'Morden Pink', *H.*'Ed Murray', *Phlox paniculata* 'Mt. Fuji', *Perovskia* sp., and *Phlox paniculata* 'Sandra'.

▲ Top to bottom: 'Tropical Glow', unnamed seedling, 'Cornwall'

◀ Daylilies in an entrance planting. Plant to left is variegated lacecap hydrangea.

▲ Massed planting of 'Stella de Oro'

▶ 'Stella de Oro' close-up

▲ Massed planting of 'Butterpat'

◄ Large container planting of 'Little Grapette' (purple), 'Butterpat' (yellow), and 'Buffys Doll' (pink)

▲ A summer border featuring daylilies in shades of one color.

▲ From center front, counterclockwise: *Hemerocallis* 'Yesterday Memories', *Nepeta* x *faasenii* 'Dropmore Purple', *Lythrum virgatum* 'Morden Pink', *Veronica* sp. 'Sunny Border Blue', and *Acanthus mollis* var. *latifolius* (hardy to Zone 6).

▶ Counterclockwise: *Hemerocallis* 'Addie Branch Smith', *H.* 'Lovely to See', *H.* 'Little Fantastic', *H.* 'Lullaby Baby', *H.* 'Beauty to Behold', with *Artemisia ludoviciana albula* 'Silver King'

▼ Top to bottom: *Lythrum* 'Morden's Pink', *Hemerocallis* 'Prairie Blue Eyes', and *H.* 'Perennial Pleasure'

▲ The white *Hemerocallis* in the front is 'Call to Remembrance' and the red, 'Tet Ed Murray'. The other whites are 'Loving Memories', 'Eternal Blessing', and 'Serene Madonna'.

◀ 'Ed Murray'

▼ 'Ed Murray' closeup

of tall, deep purple monkshood and masses of white phlox interspersed with almost any color and form of daylily. (White flowers of any sort serve as good backgrounds for the colorful daylilies and break up contrasting shades.) Many people swear by lilies (*Lilium*) as daylily companions, and their browning leaves can be hidden by the lush daylily foliage. Hostas, too, go well with them, as do perennial blue salvia, *Liatris* 'Kobold', and white and purple coneflowers. Plants with gray-green foliage such as silvery-leaved lamb's-ears, dusty miller, and 'Silvermound' artemisia are also effective complements to any color of daylily.

Avoid using invasive growers such as *Ajuga,* myrtle, low-growing sedums, and similar plants in a perennial border, or as a ground cover for daylily beds, because they can quickly take over the entire garden.

After most daylilies are past their prime, good choices for autumn bloom are the fall anemones, chrysanthemums, gloriosa daisies, 'Autumn Joy' sedum, and fall asters.

Even with the best planning and many diverse perennials, there are likely to be times in the garden when there are few blooms or none at all. Annual bedding plants are the solution. Because they flower for most of the summer, they are ideal to provide color during any dull periods. Many annuals are low growing and look good in front of the border. Such plants as ageratum, aster, alyssum, begonia, calendula, coleus, geranium, impatiens, marigold, petunia, and salvia can be planted on top of deeply set tulip or daffodil bulbs after their tops have died down. We also like both the white and pink *Lavatera,* a tall-growing mallow, for mid-to-late summer color.

In addition to choosing plants for sequence of bloom, it greatly helps the appearance of the garden if the flowers that are selected complement each other. We

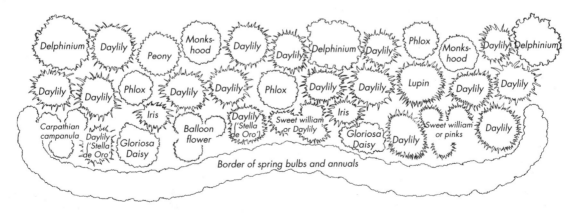

Although daylilies alone make an impressive border, in order to have bloom from spring through autumn, intersperse other perennials, as well as spring bulbs and annuals, among your daylilies.

often hear people say that color in the garden is not important, and whatever nature provides is pleasing, no matter how clashing the colors might be. This may be so in some instances, but whenever we see a carefully designed, color-coordinated planting, we are greatly impressed. The year we planted fuchsia-pink petunias next to the pale peach-colored, dwarf daylilies around a small terrace, the effect was definitely not right for a *Better Homes and Garden* centerfold. The next year we were much happier with deep purple petunias in that location. An easy way to avoid glaring clashes is to separate vibrant colors from each other with plants of white, pale pink, or pale yellow blooms. For help in making your garden completely color coordinated, seek out one of the many worthwhile books available on color in the garden.

Try to find out the approximate height of each daylily and other perennial you intend to plant. The tall plants should not hide the shorter ones, but you can create an interesting variety of textures and heights by allowing a few plants of medium height to be fairly near the front of the border. If the plants are arranged so that all the tall ones are in back, the medium in the middle, and the shorties in front, the border may look more like a set of bleacher steps than a garden. In an island planting, too, a combination of heights is more aesthetic than a tiered wedding-cake effect with the tall plants in the middle, surrounded by a circle of shorter ones, and the very lowest in front.

Plants behave differently in different locations, so even with excellent planning, it is difficult to be absolutely certain how tall a daylily or other plant will grow in your garden, or to know for sure when it will bloom. No honest-to-goodness gardeners expect their original plantings to be permanent, and the best ones shuffle their plants around frequently to get the effect they want.

Daylilies in Special Gardens

Daylilies are ideal in many types of specialty gardens. They can be used in a seasonal garden, when spring and autumn flowers are not important. Many summer residents in our community feel that daylilies give them the beauty they want for the few weeks they spend in their summer homes, and they don't need to sacrifice many vacation hours in taking care of them. Daylilies are effective in a cottage garden or a wildflower planting and, of course, no flower is more at home in a Japanese garden. They are especially good for an impatient child's first garden, and their low maintenance makes them a good choice for the elderly or partly disabled grower. Dwarf varieties are well suited for rock gardens, and many kinds are ideal for fragrant gardens (see pages 24-25, 186).

Daylilies in a Mass Planting

Long before we became interested in daylilies as a specialty, we were recommending them to customers in response to the frequently asked question, "What will grow well, need little care, and look nice on the steep slope near my home that I can't mow?"

Daylilies are ideal for covering such a bank, as well as along roadsides, pond borders, in semiwild spots, or other areas where mowing is impractical. For these types of plantings, the vigorous cultivars are the most suitable. Fortunately, most of them are not invasive, like other ground covers that spread into lawns. Also, select plants with attractive foliage that looks nice when the flowers are not in bloom.

The daylilies that best fit these requirements are not always offered by mail-order nurseries, although a local nursery can often supply them from a planting somewhere on their grounds, usually at a reasonable price. Gardening friends who are dividing their clumps are also good sources of vigorous-growing plants.

Mass plantings are most effective, as we've said, if they consist of plants of the same color rather than a mixture of many kinds. The first time we saw large masses of a single color of daylilies in bloom in a Montreal park, we were delighted at the effect. Like the famous "host of golden daffodils," the huge masses of yellow daylilies were also breathtaking, as were the plantings of all red and all pink.

Combining daylily cultivars that bloom during different seasons will ensure that there are flowers blossoming continuously in all parts of the garden over a long period. See Chapter 14 for the blooming times of many popular cultivars.

In a small mass planting, light shades show up best — yellows, beiges, pale pinks, golds, and near whites. A modest planting entirely of red or purple flowers can seem lost against a background of lawn, leaves, or evergreens. If the planting is large, however, the darker colors can be effective.

Certain kinds of cultivars are not the best choices for mass plantings. Those with blossoms of gorgeous color blends, halos, or blotches that are ideal for a mixed border can be lost in a mass planting that is ordinarily seen from a distance. Save those beauties for close-up viewing. Daily deadheading of the old blooms is impractical in a large planting, so double or ruffled flowers with thick petals are not recommended either. Such flowers are likely to hang on the plant for several days after they have faded, making the garden seem messy and unkempt.

Edging — Along the Garden Path and Elsewhere

No plants are more effective or easier to maintain along a pathway or driveway than daylilies. Their foliage acts as a neat, low hedge when the plants are not in bloom, and the blossoms are a lovely bonus. The plants are self-edgers. Because their foliage covers the border in a way that allows you to run the lawn mower up to them, no edges need to be cut around the bed, and no trimming is necessary. Daylilies can spruce up a driveway, making an entryway look "finished," and unlike shrubs, they are not damaged by piles of winter snow deposited by snowplows. They also make an excellent dividing line to define what is lawn and what is not, such as separation of a play area from the yard. Since they stay low and are competitive with other plants, they also make a good edging around a foundation planting of evergreens or flowering shrubs.

We've seen some pathway plantings of daylilies laid out like a wide garden border, and others in a simple, single row of plants. If the distance to be planted is more than 10 feet long, a variety of different cultivars adds interest; but if the distance is short, a planting of all one kind and color is more striking. Cultivars that grow less than 2 feet tall and are quite vigorous are the best choices for narrow paths, but taller ones can be used to line roadways. If they were not quite so common, the rugged Tawny Daylilies would be valued as edgings, because they are virtually indestructible and the individual flowers are attractive. For the borders of a lightly shaded woodland path, the cultivars 'Europa' and 'Kwanso' are our favorites.

Single or double rows of daylilies make effective borders around pools, decks, terraces, patios, and garden features such as sundials, wishing wells, arbors, or gazebos. They can also be effectively used to "soften" the base of a utility pole, mailbox, gas tank, or other necessary appurtenance that is not particularly attractive. We use daylilies in many such spots around our property and like the fact that they are so easy to care for.

A heavy mulch surrounds the plants, so little maintenance is necessary.

Daylilies as Foundation Plants

When faced with landscaping a home, most people think first of using evergreens and flowering shrubs. But sometimes herbaceous perennials such as daylilies, peonies, and hosta, which have fairly heavy foliage, are better choices. In areas such as ours, where winter usually brings a heavy snow cover, woody plants often suffer breakage from ice or snow that slides off roofs or is shoveled over them. Herbaceous plants that die to the ground over the winter eliminate the need for protective coverings that woody shrubs require. Since we have been using perennials as foundation plants, the 4-foot snowbanks that accumulate in the winter under our eaves don't worry us, since we know that our plants are safely tucked underground. Where heavy snows are not a problem, however, evergreens can be combined with daylilies for color during the drab, late autumn and winter months.

Daylilies are not only excellent for planting around the home, but they also fit well alongside a garage, animal barn, garden house, toolshed, or other outbuilding. In addition to adding beauty, they can soften the lines of a structure, cover an exposed foundation, and tie the building to the earth.

The north and northwest sides of a building are sometimes difficult to landscape with evergreens and flowering shrubs, because they may not get sunlight for more than an hour or two each day. Although hostas are a better choice if the shade lasts all day, most daylilies will grow in these locations if they get some sun and skylight all day long. We grow daylilies on the north and northwest sides of some of our buildings, where they get only one or two hours of low sunlight each morning and afternoon, but bright skylight the rest of the day from spring to midsummer. Compared with their siblings growing in a sunny location, the plants start to grow later in the spring, and the blooms also appear a week or so later. Still, they have been most satisfactory plants in a spot that is difficult to landscape.

If you use daylilies under a roof with no eave gutters, be careful that the rain dripping from the roof does not fall directly into the center of the clump. When you plant, set them outside the drip line or, if there is a wide overhang, in back of it, as long as you are sure they will get enough sunlight. Daylily plants beneath an over-hang may need to be watered occasionally, and those outside the drip line often need more frequent applications of fertilizer and lime than those in other locations. Even when you use a heavy mulch, the down-pours from a roof rapidly leach out the lime and nutrients in the soil.

Because most foundation plants are constantly in the limelight, choose vigor-ous daylilies with attractive blooms and healthy foliage. For best results, provide them with deep, rich soil, leave plenty of space between them so they will have room to grow (approximately 3 feet in diameter for each plant), and divide them only when they become overgrown, approximately every five to eight years. A thick mulch or one of the safer herbicides (see Chapter 7) will effectively control weeds and keep maintenance at a minimum.

Daylilies for Commercial Landscaping

The durability and low-maintenance quali-ties of daylilies make them particularly de-sirable for the landscaping of public build-ings and commercial establishments in-

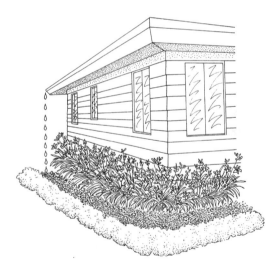

Place daylilies either inside or outside of the roof drip line, so that rain dripping from the roof does not fall directly into the center of the clumps. The eaves of this house are so deep that a bed of daylilies can be planted inside the drip line, which is lined with mulch and separates the daylilies from a narrow border of low-growing annuals outside the drip line.

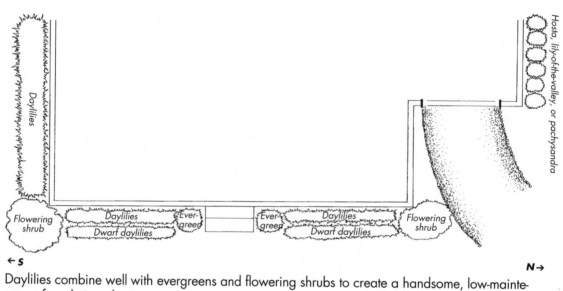

Daylilies combine well with evergreens and flowering shrubs to create a handsome, low-maintenance foundation planting.

cluding schools, banks, shopping centers, factories, motels, health-care facilities, and offices. As with home landscaping, daylilies alone can be used, or they can be combined with evergreens, flowering shrubs, and annuals.

Most nurseries are able to recommend the best cultivars for commercial landscaping. The best ones to use are those that have a long period of bloom as well as large masses of foliage that are attractive even when there are no blossoms. Sturdy kinds that grow well and form a clump quickly are also desirable, but they should not grow so rapidly that they need to be divided frequently.

Cultivars with medium to large blooms are more satisfactory than miniatures, which are not particularly showy from a distance. As with other mass plantings, cultivars with thick petals or ruffled flowers are not a good choice either because, unless their faded

blooms are picked off daily, the messy remains hang on the plants and spoil the appearance of the bed. Daily deadheading of old blooms is seldom practical in a commercial or public landscape unless gardeners are on duty all of the time.

Low-growing evergreens such as boxwood, yew, mugho pine, and juniper combine well with daylilies in a commercial planting because they provide greenery during the months of the year when the daylilies are dormant. Dwarf flowering shrubs such as daphne, spirea, and potentilla also make good companion plants in commercial landscapes because they require little maintenance. We have found that the 'Goldfinger' potentilla, which has large, yellow blooms on compact, 3-foot bushes for most of the summer, is an especially good choice.

Building a Daylily Collection

Collecting things of one sort or another is a popular hobby in our society, and plants are no exception. They may never increase in value as rapidly as coins, antique bottles, or baseball cards, but they do increase in size. Certain plant genera, especially hostas, irises, lilies, and daylilies, are especially well suited for collecting because of the vast number of varieties and cultivars available in each group.

Because more than 32,000 registered cultivars of daylilies are an overwhelming number, many collectors specialize and amass only one type of plant. Some concentrate on miniatures, and others on spiders, giants, fragrant types, species, bicolors, or those that are ruffled, eyed, or of a single color.

Probably the first step in becoming a serious daylily collector is to join the American Hemerocallis Society (see Appendix). The Society's booklets and magazines are filled with information about the different classes of daylilies, and the many nurseries that advertise in the *Daylily Journal* are good sources for all types of plants. By attending national and regional meetings you are likely to meet others with similar interests.

A daylily collection can lead you into out-of-the-way spots to find the plants of your specialty. Those who collect wild species and early hybrids, for example, search rural areas to find 'Calypso', 'Rajah', 'Valiant', 'Orangeman', and a host of others on abandoned farms or along roadsides and hedgerows. Even 'Hyperion' can be found growing completely neglected in such spots, as can species such as *Hemerocallis altissima*, *H. fulva* 'Europa', *H. middendorffii*, and of course, the early Lemon Daylily.

Labeling is crucial if you intend to collect daylilies seriously, not only in order to keep the names straight in your own mind, but also so that you can exchange plants with others with a clear conscience, knowing that you are giving them the proper cultivar. If you have a display garden, visitors will want to know the names of the plants they see, and if you do any daylily breeding, you will want to know the names of the parent plants with which you are working. For more information on the different types of labels, see Chapter 6.

If you set up a display garden, and most collectors want one after all the work and expense of collecting, it is best to plant similar cultivars and species close enough together so their differences can be easily compared. Otherwise, visitors may doubt that you actually do have 100 different spider cultivars!

Like many other gardeners, we use two types of markers to label our daylilies — a large one of plastic or wood for visitors to read, and a small, aluminum label for a more permanent marker close to the ground as insurance, in case the larger one fades or is destroyed. We also record everything in a notebook and on a computer, just in case. One year a family of young coyotes chose our daylily beds as their playground and used our large markers as teething material. The destruction was a great mystery until we finally caught them in the act.

If your beds are not on public display, the aluminum labels should be sufficient for your own uses, and without coyotes or curious youngsters around, they should last for many years.

Daylilies in Containers

If you are a gardener with only a tiny lawn or use a patio, deck, or balcony for your entire gardening space, you can grow daylilies in containers — they look at home in anything from an elegant urn to an old wooden barrel. Large clay or plastic pots, or planters built of stone, concrete, wood,

A wooden tub with adequate space for enough soil to hold the daylily's large root system makes a convenient and handsome container for a portable planting.

or landscaping ties all serve as good containers as long as they provide good drainage and room for enough soil to hold the daylily's large root system. A minimum of 10 inches in both diameter and depth is essential, and larger containers are better.

Pots that can be easily moved are especially good for decks and terraces because they can be moved in and out of prominence according to when they bloom. Plastic pots are far lighter than clay or stone for this purpose, and some of them are equally attractive.

Except for the extra-tall cultivars, nearly any daylily will look nice in a container, but for the best effect, the cultivar you select should be in proportion to the size of the planter. Miniatures are good choices for low planters, for instance, but the large-growing daylilies are better suited for big urns. The cultivars that bloom over the longest season are naturally the most satisfactory. Choose husky divisions to plant in containers, so you will get the benefit of many blooms the first year. If you pot up little plants with only one or two fans, they may have only one or two blooms, if any. We have plenty of land on our property for growing daylilies in the ground, so we don't grow daylilies permanently in containers, but we have had a great deal of experience with container growing because we grow all the plants that we sell at our nursery in pots.

Container growing is quite different from in-the-ground gardening. Weed control is easier, and the plant usually grows faster because watering and fertilizing can be more carefully controlled. Growth is likely to start earlier in the spring because the soil in containers, especially those that are dark colored, warms up faster than that in the ground, just as does soil in raised beds. Blooming is likely to begin a bit earlier for the same reason. And another plus is that it is easier to deadhead the old blooms because the plants are higher off the ground and easier to reach.

There are minuses, too. Any plant growing in a container is more demanding than one growing in the ground. The soil dries out rapidly when it has no contact with the moisture in the earth, so unless it rains, the plant needs watering every day during the growing season. Plants in clay pots may need watering twice a day, in fact, because the soil dries out faster in clay pots. Unless you have automatic watering, long weekends away are out of the question. Also, the frequent waterings rapidly leach plant nutrients and lime from the soil, so frequent but light applications of these are the rule, as opposed to the once-a-year feedings most of us provide for our plants in the ground.

Soil for Containers

Most gardeners who grow plants in containers have a favorite soil mix, and if you already have one that you feel provides good results with similar plants, you should also use it for daylilies. Some people buy commercial potting soil, but others prefer to mix their own. The usual formula for a good container mix is a 1:1:1 proportion by volume: one-third good topsoil, one-third sharp river sand (sand that is clean and not too fine), and one-third humus. Perlite, which is extremely lightweight, can be substituted for the sand, and this is a good choice if you plan to move the pots frequently. The humus used most often is peat moss, because it is available in most garden stores, but it works just as well to use either sifted compost, aged manure, composted leaves or bark, or a combination of these organic products.

An artificial soil mix such as Gro-Mix or Metro Mix has the advantage of being free of disease and weeds, but these mixes sometimes contain too much humus for the pots to drain well. When we use one, we combine it with a little sand or perlite so that it will not retain more water than is good for the plants.

If you use commercial potting soil especially formulated for container plants, choose one that contains composted manure or bark. These supply a generous amount of nutrients in their natural form which gives them an advantage over artificial mixes, and since they are organic, the nutrients don't leach away as quickly as those in chemical fertilizers.

Careful fertilizing is crucial to the good health of any container-grown plants, including daylilies. The amount of soil in a container is so small that any common dry-chemical garden fertilizer, such as 5-10-10, must be added in very small amounts to avoid burning the plant. Organic fertilizers, such as dried manure or seaweed, are good choices because they act slowly, and an accidental overdose does not burn the plants. Slow-acting fertilizers, such as Mag-Amp or Osmocote, also release their nutrients slowly and thus are safer than the more soluble chemicals, but some growers in warmer areas have reported that it is dangerous to use them when temperatures are high. The slow-release ingredients apparently become more activated in the heat, causing a sudden release of nitrogen, which can harm the plants.

Some gardeners prefer to use liquid fertilizers exclusively, either by applying a weak solution every week or a stronger one whenever the plant appears to need more nourishment. We, however, prefer to mix a slow-acting organic fertilizer into the soil at planting time, and add a liquid plant food only when the plants appear to need it.

Daylilies need the trace element magnesium for good growth, so when feeding them, whether they are in pots or in the ground, try to use a fertilizer that includes it, as well as the usual nitrogen, potassium,

and phosphorus. If the fertilizer does not contain it, you can easily supply it with an annual watering of a solution consisting of 1 tablespoon of Epsom salts per gallon of water, or a sprinkling of dolomitic limestone.

In a warm climate, it works well to leave the daylilies in their containers on top of the ground all winter as long as you water them occasionally so they never dry out completely. In the North, you can leave the plants outdoors on top of the ground if *(a)* you are growing hardy, dormant plants, *(b)* the planter has no bottom or has a large hole in the bottom so that it maintains contact with the earth, and *(c)* the container is low enough so that snow will cover most of it during the coldest part of the winter. Unless all three of these conditions are met, precautions are necessary. Even when the roots are not damaged by freezing, drainage holes in a pot become useless when the soil freezes, and on warm days, melting snow or spring rains fill the upper part of the pot with water for long periods.

To store container-grown daylilies over winter, place containers in a sheltered place, tip them on their sides, pack them close together, and cover them with boughs or other insulating material. These plants will be completely covered by the pine boughs.

To prevent damage from cold and possible drowning of the plants, place the containers in a sheltered place after the foliage has died back in the fall. Tip them on their sides, pack them close together on the ground, and cover them with boughs or other insulating material. Dig up any plants growing in urns or containers that are too large to move, plant them in the ground before it freezes, and mulch them heavily. In the spring, dig and repot them after hard frosts are over.

Because plants in containers are likely to grow rapidly, they need more frequent dividing than would be necessary if they were in the ground. Gardeners in areas that are nearly frost free, such as Florida and southern California, usually need to divide their container-grown daylilies annually. In the North, division once every two or three years is usually sufficient, depending on the vigor of the plant and size of the pot.

Daylilies Illuminated

Some of the nocturnal daylilies open in early evening and stay open throughout the night, and many diurnal daylilies stay in bloom until ten o'clock or later. If you have many such "flowers of the night," you may want to install lights in the garden so that you and your friends can enjoy them. An extra bonus of visiting the garden after dark is that the fragrance of most flowers, including daylilies, is often more pronounced in the evening.

Flowers do not look the same under artificial lights as they do in daylight. Gaslights and kerosene torches affect the colors considerably, and different types of electric lighting — incandescent, fluorescent, mercury, and quartz — accentuate different shades. You may want to experiment with various kinds in your garden or observe a neighbor's system before choosing your type of lighting.

Solar-operated lights can be used to illuminate small gardens, pools, or other features of large gardens. These are handy because they eliminate not only the need for wiring, but also the nuisance of turning them on and off. Most shine for only a few hours after dark, so their use is limited, but when skillfully placed, they can be a happy addition to an evening landscape.

Skilled outdoor-lighting engineers are expensive and not available in many locations, but you can experiment, using their methods. Place a few lights behind shrubs on the ground, or conceal them on poles behind tall shrubs or trees, and move them from place to place on a dark night until you discover what is most effective for illuminating the garden. The source of outdoor lighting is most effective if the lights themselves are not visible, and of course, they shouldn't shine into the viewer's eyes.

Daylilies as Food

Westerners have not been conditioned to think of beautiful daylilies as vegetables. If they were not quite as attractive, we might more willingly eat them. But they have been a source of food for centuries in the Orient, where gardeners grow them as an edible cash crop. Dried daylily flowers are found in Chinese food stores all over North America, and we were recently delighted when friends brought us a package from Chinatown in Montreal. The transliterated name in English is Gum Jum or Kam Cham, which means "golden needle"; or Gum Tsoy which means "golden vegetable." The

dried, withered flowers appear more faded brown than golden to us in appearance, but their taste can be "golden."

All parts of the plant are edible. The abundant 'Europa' and vigorous 'Dumortieri' can be dug in late spring for their newly sprouted white roots, which resemble tubers. When eaten raw, their texture resembles that of a radish, and the flavor is nutlike, somewhat sweet, and similar to that of a water chestnut. Chinese chefs cook the roots in a wide variety of ways and like the fact that the texture remains crisp, even after cooking. They are high in protein, low in fat, and rich in a variety of other minerals and vitamins.

The entire crown of a daylily plant can also be used for food; it should be cut off just as it begins to grow rapidly in early summer but before the flower scapes appear. Strip off the outer leaves and use the center, either cut up raw in salads or cooked like asparagus.

If you have a hillside covered with 'Europa' or other vigorous plants, they will probably grow faster than you can harvest them, whether you scoop out the crowns of a few or nibble their roots. A patch of fast-growing daylilies can be a tasty insurance against a food shortage and, like Jerusalem artichokes, provide a sure-to-grow, high-quality, low-starch food.

Most of us settle for eating the buds. All varieties of commonly grown daylily flowers are edible, and experimentation will help you find the flavors you like best. Most daylily gourmets agree that the pinks, yellows, and oranges are better flavored than the reds and other dark colors, which taste somewhat bitter. Varieties with a strong scent have a stronger, sweeter flavor.

The flowers are edible from the time the buds form until one day after they have faded. The first day after flowering is the time many people prefer their flavor, but the second day they become bitter. Although the faded blooms do not look as appe-

---

The American Daylily Society provides the following information about the nutritive value of daylilies compared with a few other vegetables:

Vegetable	Vitamin C (mg/100g)	Vitamin A (IU)	% protein
Daylily buds	43	983	3.1
Asparagus	33	1000	2.2
Okra	30	740	1.8
String beans	19	630	2.4

tizing as the fresh buds, it doesn't matter if you plan to cook them, and you'll have the pleasure of seeing the opened blossom, as well.

When you have picked the buds or flowers, wash them, and if you're using the opened flowers, remove the stamens and pistil. If you are using dried Gum Jum in cooking, simply soak them for a minimum of a half-hour to reconstitute the dehydrated flowers, and then use them as you would if they had been fresh.

One of the easiest ways to enjoy the buds or flowers is to cut them fresh into salads. They spice up the appearance as well as the flavor of an ordinary green salad; or you can chop them and add them to soups, casseroles, omelets or scrambled eggs. Some cooks fry the buds after dipping them into an egg batter and rolling them in flour and seasonings. Others sauté them by simply salting them and placing them in a covered fry pan over low heat until the moisture is removed. We sometimes boil them for about five minutes in chicken broth or bouillon and serve them with butter, salt, and pepper.

Both buds and roots can be frozen for future use. Simply blanch them in hot water for three minutes and chill them quickly under cold water. Then drain and pack them in freezer bags or cartons.

As a garnish, daylily flowers are spectacular. It is difficult to imagine a more beautiful way to serve chicken salad at a summer luncheon, for example, than to scoop individual portions into the center of large, beautiful daylilies, each of a different shade.

You will find recipe suggestions in books on Chinese cookery, where Gum Jum may be called "Tiger Lilies," or in a flower cookbook. Our favorite is *The Forgotten Art of Flower Cookery* by Keiba Woodring Smith (New York: Harper and Row, 1973), which we found at a library book sale. It has many pages of recipes that use daylilies.

Daylilies not only have nutritive qualities, but they also have traditionally been valued by Orientals for medicinal uses. Daylily roots are considered to have pain-killing and diuretic properties and have been used in the treatment of a variety of ailments, including fevers, breast tumors, dropsy, hemorrhoids, and jaundice.

Daylilies may never become a staple in the North American diet, but they can be a happy addition to your culinary repertoire. You have only to go as far as your backyard.

CHAPTER 5

Selecting the Best Daylilies for Your Garden

IT IS ABSURD to imagine that anyone could tell anyone else how to appreciate flowers, since beauty is, as the saying goes, in the eyes of the beholder. But there are different ways of seeing. We have discovered that it is easy to become overwhelmed by the profusion of beauty and variety when standing in the midst of a large, multicolored garden or field of daylilies. It takes effort to see beyond the mass display and closely scrutinize individual flowers, like the difference between walking briskly through an art gallery, getting an impressive overview of the size, variety, and colors of the many paintings and sauntering slowly past a few special masterpieces, taking the time to appreciate their intricacies and particular characteristics. A satisfying tour of any garden encompasses both kinds of viewing.

If you have difficulty making up your mind, choosing new daylilies is no easy feat, as we know from experience. Years ago,

when we bought our first plants, there existed only a tiny fraction of the 32,000 plus cultivars registered today by the American Hemerocallis Society, but even then we couldn't decide which ones to buy. We felt just as we do when we buy carrot seed: no matter which we choose, there is a nagging feeling that we might be missing something better.

It is interesting to watch how the different customers in our nursery select daylilies when they're in bloom. Some wander around the sales yard and randomly pick out plants that catch their eye. Others, more choosy, want only a certain color and ignore all the rest. Some look only for miniature varieties for a rock garden. Still others spend hours sniffing to find the most fragrant or seek out the night bloomers because they entertain in their garden on summer nights. People who raise flowers entirely for arrangements want only those with sturdy blooms that hold up well in bouquets. And some choose impulsively, according to a tempting name: 'Hot Toddy', for a friend who imbibes; 'Princess Irene', for a sister by that name; or 'Disneyland', to recall a vacation in California the previous winter.

When we first shopped for daylilies, the blossom was the only thing that mattered. We acquired them according to how much we liked the flowers on a scale of one to ten, if we could afford them. After years of buying plants, however, we have become more discriminating, and when we find a beautiful flower we look for other qualities as well, such as the plant's hardiness, vigor, how many buds it produces, and how long it continues to blossom. We also want to know the time of year it blooms, whether early, mid-season, or late, since we want day-lilies over a long season. These attributes are often listed in catalog descriptions, or you can determine many of them for yourself by observation when you visit a nursery.

Before you begin to shop for plants, it is helpful to analyze what you expect from your planting. If you need to cover a bank of poor, gravel-filled soil, you should choose quite different plants than you would for a showy backyard border. If you have lots of room and intend to plant masses of showy daylilies, you will need different types than you'd choose for three clumps near the back door. The listing of plants in chapters 14 and 15 can help you make your selections. You will find cultivars classified according to such things as blooming time and flower form, as well as lists of those that have become popular. Don't use the

Beginner's Selection

The following are our choices for a small collection of attractive, vigorous, and easy-to-grow daylilies. There are undoubtedly hundreds of others just as worthwhile, but these have been grown over a wide area of North America for many years and thrive in most gardens in the North Temperate Zone.

Yellow and Gold
Decatur Moonlight
Green Flutter
Green Ice
Hudson Valley
Hyperion
Prairie Moonlight
Susan Elizabeth
Winning Ways

Red
Chicago Brave
Chicago Rosy
Ed Murray

Orchid and Purple
Grape Harvest
Royal Quest
Russian Rhapsody
Sugar Candy

Orange
George Cunningham
Manila Moon
Outrageous
Passing By
Polka Time

Pink
Computer
Fabulous Flame
Fairy Tale Pink
Neyron Rose
Pink Snow Flakes
Pink Swan
Precious One

Near White
Call to Remembrance
Guardian Angel
Hope Diamond

lists as if they were the last word, though. There are thousands of wonderful daylilies that are not on any lists.

Hardy Plants for Northern Gardens

Gardeners in Zones 3, 4, and 5 need to be sure that the plants they select are hardy in their climate. As a general rule, only those with dormant foliage are considered reliably hardy. If you live in Zone 5 or colder zones and want to try evergreen or semi-evergreen daylilies in your garden, try to get them from a northern nursery rather than one in California or Louisiana. There is no guarantee that an evergreen daylily sold in the Midwest will be better suited to a Minnesota garden than one grown in Alabama, but as long as the Midwest nursery grows its own plants and does not import them from a wholesaler in the South, the chances are better for the evergreen's survival.

Daylilies, like other perennials, survive a winter better if the temperature stays cold for most of the winter after it drops in the autumn. If there are frequent periods when the ground thaws for a few days and then freezes again, plants that are not acclimated suffer badly.

Native plants are acclimated to whatever conditions exist in their area and seldom suffer damage from the cold. Like the mythical Persephone, they go underground for the winter. As the days shorten in late summer, they stop growing, the nourishment in the leaves returns to the roots, and the plants become dormant before ground-freezing frosts can harm them.

Plants that originated in areas with longer growing seasons often have trouble adjusting to a different cycle of seasons, and they may continue to grow until late in the autumn, just as they would in their native environment. Consequently, their cells, which are alive and full of moisture, rupture and the plant dies.

Unlike magnolia, pecan, and fig trees, which don't die back to the ground in the winter and will probably never become acclimated to a cold climate, daylilies and other perennials can often adjust their growing habits to a new climate if they can be kept alive for a few years with protection. For this reason, we often see tender evergreen daylilies growing in northern gardens. This is especially true of those cultivars that were created by crossing a dormant or semi-evergreen with an evergreen.

If you are unable to find the plants you want in a nursery near you and need to order from a southern establishment, ask to have them shipped in the spring rather than in late summer or fall. This timing will give your newcomers an entire growing season to adjust to their new conditions and to develop a sturdy root system before the first frosts. Plan to mulch the plant heavily for the first few winters, according to the directions in Chapter 7. With a little puttering and tender care you may be able to grow an outstanding evergreen that will be hardy.

Northern gardeners often find that the late-blooming daylily cultivars are not as satisfactory as they might be in another location where the climate provides a long, frost-free autumn. Our first frost usually arrives soon after Labor Day, and as we have said, even before that time, when the thermometer drops to 40°F. at night, the blooms in our garden only partially open the following day. The late bloomers are not a complete failure for us, however. The buds are remarkably frost resistant, and even after several hard frosts in early September, the weather often warms again and the daylilies bloom beautifully.

Dormants in Southern Gardens

Gardeners in the South who want to grow dormant cultivars usually have no trouble. Still, a few kinds prefer a northern home and probably will never perform at their best in the South even though they may not actually die. Southern growers are fortunate because so many breeders live in the South that the evergreen hybrids introduced each year now outnumber the dormants and usually surpass them in color quality. A high percentage of the leading award-winning plants in recent years have been evergreens. Fortunately for all sections of the country, many hybridizers now try to combine the hardiness of dormants with the beauty of evergreens, and many of these do well in both the North and South.

Buying Plants by Mail

Daylily catalogs certainly live up to their reputation as "wish books." Their gorgeous, mouth-watering colored photos make us want to reach for our checkbook immediately and order one from every page. Daylily plants are sold by seed and nursery companies that carry a wide assortment of trees and plants, by large nurseries that sell mostly daylilies, and by small firms that carry only a limited number of plants, sometimes only their own introductions.

Because general nurseries do not specialize in daylilies, their plant selection is understandably more limited than that of nurseries that specialize in daylilies. The plants are likely to be older varieties, too, and some firms sell plants according to color rather than by cultivar name. For the casual gardener, these may be perfectly satisfactory, but if you are more discriminating and want the best cultivars, it is better to get them from a catalog of a firm that specializes in daylilies. (See Appendix for a list of mail-order nurseries.)

The plants offered by large daylily nurseries often offer the best mail-order choices for new gardeners. Large firms are most likely to offer "commercial-type" daylilies that are vigorous, clump up fast, and are suitable for growing over a wide part of the country. Small mail-order firms tend to specialize mostly in high-quality, prize-winning plants that are likely to be found on lists of the 100 favorite daylilies. The newer introductions are also likely to be found in their lists.

Daylily catalogs vary a great deal. Some provide good pictures and detailed information about the plants. Others, which offer little more than a plant's name, are useful only to knowledgeable growers who know exactly what they want. Beware of firms that list only a plant's good points with superlatives that would have pleased P. T. Barnum, but leave it up to you to figure out all the things left unsaid.

The most helpful daylily catalog descriptions give the scape height, the size and form of bloom, and blooming time. They state whether the plant is dormant, semi-evergreen, or evergreen, the name of the originator, date of introduction, and the awards it has won, if any. The daylily is described often so enticingly that in reading through the listing alphabetically each year, by the time we have reached "B" our entire daylily budget is exhausted, and we have run out of allotted garden space.

Even though a picture may be worth a thousand words, we have learned to care-fully compare photos with the plant descriptions. The coloring of the daylilies often becomes changed considerably during the process of photographing and printing.

Choosing Plants from a Nursery or Garden Center

A visit to a display garden or daylily nursery at blooming time is one of the best ways to decide which cultivars you like and to make comparisons. With thousands of plants available, you can be quite certain that many are very much alike. At a nursery, you can compare flowers and see them actually growing in clumps, and if the nursery is nearby, you can be reasonably assured that the plants will be suitable for growing in your climate. If you can visit at different times, you'll be able to select a variety of plants that will provide blooms throughout the season.

We like to visit nurseries when the daylilies are in bloom for the reasons given above, as well as to compare the flowers with catalog descriptions and pictures. When a catalog states that a flower is "pink," it is hard to know which of dozens of shades of pink the writer had in mind. Also, at a nursery we can look over the plant as closely as the flowers, a

Nursery-grown potted daylilies are a good choice because they become established and begin to bloom heavily a full year earlier than bare-rooted plants.

lesson we've taken to heart after buying a few that were disappointingly weak and changed little after several years of tender care. Some of the best near-whites we fell for had only a bloom or two in the several years we nursed them along, so we finally, sadly, tossed them out.

The type of plant we look for produces many buds and has healthy foliage. If we are searching for red cultivars, we try to get those with blooms that don't fade in the hot sun, as reds sometimes have a tendency to do. It is easy, however, to get carried away with a pretty bloom, and it takes concentration to keep all the other desirable factors in mind when we are suddenly faced with hundreds of different cultivars.

As we have come to know daylilies better, we have become more discriminating and notice fine points that wouldn't have been important to us earlier. The substance of the petals, for instance, makes a difference. We try to select cultivars with moderately heavy petals because some of our earlier acquisitions are so fragile that the petals break in a light breeze or whenever we pick them for a bouquet. We notice characteristics we were only mildly aware of before, including pie-crust edgings and the delightful gold or silvery diamond dusting.

If the nursery sells potted daylilies, they are a good choice because they can become established and begin to bloom heavily a full year earlier than bare-rooted ones. The plants are usually a bit more expensive, and unfortunately the variety of cultivars available in pots is likely to be limited. Many nurseries dig plants while you wait and wrap them in newspaper or pop them in a paper bag. Although we have had success setting out such plants, they always take longer than potted plants to recover from the transplant shock and begin growing.

Many nurseries have display gardens where you can see mature specimens of the plants that they sell. Others let you see the stock plants from which they get their propagation material. These give you a better idea of how your purchases will look when they are fully grown, because a full-grown plant looks quite different from a small plant with only a blossom or two in the sales area. Display gardens can also give you a chance to look at plants the nursery does not have for sale every year, for future reference.

Old Standbys versus the Very Newest

The prices for daylilies are based almost entirely on supply and demand rather than upon their quality, so a $200 plant is not automatically twenty times better than one that costs $10. Unlike tea roses and fruit trees, daylilies can be easily propagated by anyone, so they are not patented. The originator must charge a high price for a new cultivar in order to recover expenses and to make a profit quickly before other nurseries have a chance to propagate and sell it, too.

The price sometimes stays high for several years, however, because many of the most popular hybrids lack the vigor of older varieties, so they can't be propagated rapidly. They also stay expensive for a long time if they are in great demand. Dance Ballerina Dance, a large, lovely pink ruffled cultivar, stayed in the $50 price range for many years before it dropped into the $25 class.

Because supply is the factor that determines price, the cost of the same cultivar may vary considerably at different nurseries. For this reason, if you are buying an expensive daylily, you may want to compare its price at several different sources.

When we first planted daylilies in the 1940s, we paid less than a dollar for each one, so it is shocking for us to find plants listed in catalogs today in the price range of $3 to over $200. The high price of a new plant that is for the most part still unproven causes a lot of grumbling among daylily fans at garden club meetings. One woman reported that when one of her $100 daylily plants died, her husband was so upset that he made her have a funeral for it! When you invest in the very latest model of anything — a car, a camera, or a daylily — you are taking a chance. You may end up with a delightful product, or you may find several "bugs" if it has not been thoroughly tested over time. A number of letters to the editors of garden magazines contain complaints that some of the new daylily introductions do not live up to their descriptions.

Another common complaint that buyers have about expensive new plants is that some originators, anxious to get the fastest return, ship tiny plants that take many years to bloom. On more than one occasion we have bought an expensive new hybrid and found to our dismay that four years later it still consisted of only one bloomless fan, no larger than when we bought it. Overhybridizing often weakens a plant, and when breeders concentrate on producing prize-winning blooms, beauty often takes precedence over plant vigor and other important qualities. We have learned that it doesn't always pay to be the "first kid on your block" with a new cultivar. If you wait patiently a few years, the bad points of a plant become known; and if the cultivar proves to be a winner, very likely the price will drop to a reasonable figure. Since several hundred new introductions appear in some years, it is obvious that only a few will become well known nationally, and many of today's sensations are doomed to be forgotten.

Who buys most of the expensive plants? Skeptics say it is usually breeders who use them to start other expensive plants! Of course, this is an exaggeration. All of us have a bit of gambler's blood and want to experiment. There is something very satisfying about owning a daylily that may turn out to be the best plant of the decade. Many new introductions are stunningly beautiful and truly superior plants. Just be forewarned that high prices do not always mean high quality.

Award-winning Daylilies

You would think that any daylily that wins an award would be the best of the lot, and often this is the case. (See the list of award winners in Chapter 13.) Each has been chosen a winner for a good reason. However, daylily judges look for extremely fine points that usually do not matter much to ordinary gardeners. They may pay more attention to flower form than plant vigor and disease resistance, for instance.

You may want to choose award-winning cultivars for their beauty or some of their other fine qualities, but keep in mind that there are thousands of superior daylilies growing around North America that most of the judges have never seen, none of which has ever won a national award or made the "top 100" list. They may be, nevertheless, of award-winning caliber and ideal for a backyard garden. We suggest that you buy the daylilies you truly admire, whether or not the judges have rated them as winners. Although we greatly admire both the dedicated breeders who develop the beautiful new hybrids and those who judge them, in our own garden we have the final word.

Is She, or Is She Not My Baby?

Receiving plants that are mislabeled is a frustrating experience for a gardener, but it happens to most of us sooner or later. When you receive a dormant plant in the mail or buy a cultivar not in bloom at a nursery, there's no way of knowing whether or not it is the one you thought you were getting until it blossoms. Even then, if it closely resembles the description of the one you ordered, you can't be sure. Of course, when you receive a plant labeled "Red Cardinal Supreme" and the flowers turn out to be dull yellow, there is strong reason to suspect that something is not right.

Mislabeled plants are almost always the result of careless labeling at the nursery, rather than a deliberate replacement for a cultivar that they no longer had. Growers must often hire unskilled workers during the busy digging and shipping seasons, and mistakes happen. Even in a garden center or a small nursery like ours, plants become mislabeled when customers pull out a label, read it, and then inadvertently return it to the wrong pot.

Recently, mislabeled daylilies have appeared on the market because nurseries have put too much trust in modern technology. For the past few years, berry plants, orchids, and fruit-tree stocks have been routinely propagated by tissue culture — the test-tube method of producing plants by the millions in a laboratory. A few large wholesale nurseries also use tissue culture to rapidly reproduce in large numbers popular daylilies such as 'Stella de Oro' and 'Dance Ballerina Dance'. Unfortunately, the results have not always been carefully monitored, and occasionally the plants have mutated in the artificial environment. Consequently, thousands of so-called 'Stella de Oro' were sold in garden centers all over the country, but they were not 'Stella de Oro'; and the same mutation has occurred with other popular cultivars.

Some garden center and nursery owners conscientiously check their shipments of tissue-cultured daylilies by growing the young plants to blooming size before selling them, thus verifying that they are true to name. There have been so many complaints about "in vitro" blunders, however, that some retail outlets now proudly advertise that they do not sell tissue-cultured daylilies.

Whenever possible, buy the cultivars you want when you can see them in bloom at a local nursery. Since this is not always feasible, try to deal with a reputable nursery, and let them know when you are certain that you have received plants other than the ones you ordered.

Plants from Other Sources

If you don't mind growing daylilies that are not named cultivars, there are other ways to increase the size of your collection. One way is to buy seeds and grow your own. A few companies (see Appendix) offer both diploid and tetraploid seed, as do certain large growers and hybridizers.

Whenever you discover choice beauties in your own daylily collection, you may want to cross-pollinate them and then collect and plant the seed. There's an excellent chance that you will raise some beauties that are quite different from their parents (see chapters 9 and 10 for instructions).

If any daylily hybridizers work in your area, they may have quantities of fine seedling plants that don't measure up to their high standards for naming and introduction, and they often sell them at reasonable prices. A good percentage of these seedlings are likely to be better than many named varieties. The late Reverend Dr. Barth of Alna, Maine, became well known for his "Daylily Day," scheduled each year on the last Saturday of July. He opened his fields to hundreds of people, offering dozens of clumps of "bargain daylilies" which were leftovers from his breeding experiments. The proceeds of the event went to local civic organizations. The members did the advertising and digging, and served food for this much-anticipated town holiday. Dr. Barth's fields were then left clean and ready for his experimentation the following year.

There are probably many other sources for plants in your area. Daylilies multiply quickly, and in every neighborhood there are thousands of clumps of wonderful cultivars that need dividing. Most gardeners, especially daylily enthusiasts, enjoy exchanging plants, so if you have some good kinds to swap, you can probably work out trades with fellow gardeners that will make all of you very happy.

Community fairs and plant sales can also be sources of daylilies, and occasionally even at yard sales there are a few clumps boxed or potted up to decorate the merchandise area. Garden club members often earn money for projects by dividing their plants, which are likely to be of high quality.

Use normal gardener's caution when you accept gift plants or buy them at a plant sale. It is easy to bring home both unwelcome insects and obnoxious weeds. Diseases, too, tend to be stowaways among roots and foliage. If you are even slightly suspicious that your new daylily may be a

Trojan horse, wash the entire plant, including all the soil from the roots, and keep it in a quarantine area for a few weeks before planting it in your garden.

Keeping Records

The more you know about each of your daylilies the more interesting it is. One way to collect information and refer to it quickly is to use file cards. Make out a card for each cultivar, noting its parents if you can, the date of introduction, originator, foliage (dormant, evergreen, etc.), and whether it is nocturnal, fragrant, an extended bloomer, rebloomer, or a tetraploid, and give a general description of the plant and flower. Note the year you bought it and from whom, the price paid, where it is planted, and add any year-by-year comments on its performance.

CHAPTER 6

Preparing the Soil and Planting

IF YOU WANT TO GROW the new daylily cultivars at their best, forget the statement that daylilies will thrive anywhere, even in poor soil. Gardeners who have grown only the older cultivars like 'Rajah', 'Imperator', or 'Orangeman', which flourish like weeds no matter where they are planted, often assume that all daylilies have the same potential. Most modern cultivars are more delicate, however. Flowers as beautiful as 'Decatur Rhythm' or 'Strawberry Rose' deserve soil conditions as good as those you would provide for a delphinium or carnation.

Modern daylilies are certainly not as fussy about the pH and quality of the soil as heather or mountain laurel, but they do best if it is to their liking. Because the plants have very deep roots, they grow best, bloom best, and can better withstand a dry summer heat when they reside in deep, fertile soil.

We used to hear that you should never put a $10 tree into a $1 hole. The figures need readjustment for some of today's day-

lilies, but the theory is still correct: a special plant needs special care to get it off to a good start.

When to Plant

The old rule for planting perennials used to be that above the Mason-Dixon line, springtime was best; below it, autumn was equally good, and perhaps better. Recently, nurseries and professional gardeners have debunked this theory, and advertisements frequently indicate that autumn is a good time to plant anywhere. Whether autumn planting is always good for plants in the North is debatable, however. A cynic might say that it is definitely good for the nursery business.

In the South you can safely set out bare-rooted daylilies just about any time of the year that nurseries will sell them, although the results are more likely to be better when the weather is cool and damp, rather than in the dry heat of summer.

Many gardeners traditionally divide their overgrown daylilies in late summer, after they stop blooming, and immediately plant the divisions. This works well in most of the country, but in Zones 3 and 4, where frosts come in early September, the new plants may not become established enough to survive the winter before the ground begins to freeze. Moving undivided clumps with a ball of soil can be done safely almost any time of the year if they are kept watered, but in Zone 3 we do not like to plant small divisions and mail-order plants after mid-August. Potted daylilies from a garden center can be planted safely just about any time that the ground isn't frozen.

Most northern gardeners have found that it is safest to plant mail-order plants in the spring. Occasionally, when a cultivar is especially scarce and the nursery will ship it only in September or October, we plant it in a cold frame covered with a thick layer of leaves or evergreen boughs. Protected in this way it usually survives very well, starting to sprout up through the mulch by the time we want to transplant it to its permanent location after the weather warms up in spring.

Locating the Planting Site

Choosing the best spot to plant your daylilies is not as critical a decision as it is for many other plants, because most daylilies are not as fussy about soil pH and sun conditions. Also, daylily scapes are so sturdy that they seldom need staking to hold up their big load of heavy blooms or to protect them from the wind. As with all plants, however, some locations are better choices than others.

As we have said, most *Hemerocallis* cultivars grow best in full sunlight, but if the spot receives a half day of full sun, and skylight for the remainder of the day, they will thrive. Our perennial garden is shaded in early morning by the house and again in late afternoon by a 6-foot arborvitae hedge, but the plants do well anyway. Avoid setting most kinds underneath trees where sunlight is scarce. Only a few daylilies — certain species and early cultivars — will grow in the shade of trees, and even then the shade should not be too dense. In spots that are heavily shaded, different varieties of hosta are much more satisfactory.

Daylilies planted near trees or large shrubs not only suffer from too much shade, but also from root competition. Since there is about as much of a tree under the surface of the ground as there is above, a contest for water and nutrients is always going on between the tree's massive roots and neighboring plants. Only the rugged, older species of daylilies can meet this kind of challenge successfully, so choose these or closely related varieties (see page 28) if you want to encircle the trunk of a tree or plant them near a vigorous growing hedge.

Gardeners in villages or suburbs must be aware of their neighbors' trees as well as their own. Not only do large trees present problems, but small trees grow, and the spot that is a sunny bed when you plant the daylilies may be in deep shade within a few years.

The blooms of certain cultivars tend to face the sun, like sunflowers, so it is a good idea to determine the sun's position in relation to your garden. This positioning is not as important for early-summer bloomers, because at that time of year the sun is high in the sky and provides a great deal of light in all directions. When you have many late-summer bloomers, however, plan your garden so viewers will be looking at the flowers head-on rather than at the backs of the blooms. Of course, if a tall hedge, building, solid fence, or wall is in the background, the flowers will naturally turn toward the front of the garden anyway, so there will be no problem.

Designing a Planting

Although daylilies will provide an impressive display even if you plant them haphazardly all around a property, a well-organized garden or landscaped planting is far more satisfactory. Whenever many different cultivars are planted together without a plan, the effect in future years is likely to show it: dwarf-growing cultivars will be buried among large ones; vigorous growers will crowd the weaker ones; late-flowering plants may be clustered together, making the rest of the garden devoid of blooms during that season; and the colors are likely to be so uncoordinated that vivid reds and oranges "swear violently" at each other.

In a wild-type garden you might want a casual, unplanned effect, but in your backyard border it is not likely to be attractive. It is easy to remedy such a situation and prevent a lot of backbreaking moving later on by making a plan before planting, either informally in your head, or better yet, on graph paper, keeping in mind different daylily sizes, colors, vigor, and time of bloom.

Soil Preparation

Preparing the soil for planting new daylilies is little different than getting ready to plant a vegetable garden, perennial bed, or strawberry patch, so if you are already a gardener, you may want to skip this section.

When planting in the spring, wait until the soil is dry enough to till or spade it. Otherwise you will be compacting the wet soil more than loosening it. The usual method of determining whether or not the soil is dry enough for working is to squeeze a handful. If it stays compact after releasing it, it is too moist, and you should let it dry out a bit more.

Soils in most areas of North America have been used and misused for so many years, it is difficult to find any that won't benefit from one treatment or another. Check out the condition of your beds before you plant anything, because it is far easier to correct any shortcomings before you plant rather than after. If the soil is very heavy, for example, you will need to add sand and extra humus to lighten it so the plant roots can easily grow.

Daylilies have deep roots and are "heavy feeders," which means that they need more moisture and nutrients than pansies or primula. If you are setting out several individual plants in different spots, dig a large hole for each one, 2 feet in diameter and at least 18 inches in depth. Mix fertilizer and humus with the soil you remove, before setting the plant and refilling the hole. A shovelful of homemade compost or other humus per hole should be adequate.

When planting large areas, such as a hillside where you don't want to loosen up a lot of soil that could wash away, digging a hole for each plant is often a better solution than tilling the entire area. Since you will be using vigorous kinds of daylilies for planting in such a location, it may not be necessary to do any soil enrichment if the soil is in fairly good shape. It is good insurance, nevertheless, to add a small amount of humus to each hole before you plant, and to fertilize around the daylilies after they are planted.

Beds of more refined daylilies deserve more refined treatment. If you are preparing an entire bed, till or spade it thoroughly to a depth of at least 18 inches or, as many gardeners prefer, 2 feet if soil conditions will permit it. If you have aged farm manure available, work it into the soil, or use your own compost or commercially composted leaves or bark, dried manure, peat moss, or other organic matter. It is difficult to know for sure what is the proper amount of humus-producing material to apply. Obvi-

ously, if your soil is already fairly good, it will take less than if it is in poor shape. One wheelbarrow load (4 cubic feet) spread over 50 square feet is about right for average soil, and more is helpful if the soil is poor. In a lecture to a garden club, long ago, when we recommended old cow manure, one woman asked thoughtfully, "How old does the cow need to be?" Now I am careful to say "well-aged" but still feel that it is one of the best plant foods you can use. Manure isn't always easy to come by any more, though, because not only are dairy farms scarce in many areas, but farmers are less likely to part with such a valuable resource. Sheep and rabbit manure are also good, and these can be rototilled into the soil even if they are fresh. Horse owners often have a surplus of manure, but horse, as well as pig and poultry manures "heat" as they age, and if they are mixed fresh with the soil at planting time, they are likely to damage the plants' roots. Compost these hot manures first, or spread them on top of the soil in late fall as a mulch. If you decide to mulch with them, however, don't let them touch the plants.

Shavings and chips are fine to use as mulch, but when they are mixed with the soil, they deplete the nitrogen content. The bacteria that are necessary for decaying wood products need a great deal of nitrogen for the process, and naturally it is taken from the soil at the expense of the plants. If these products are the only source of humus available, or if they are already in the soil, it is important to add a fertilizer containing more than the usual amount of nitrogen. Fertilizing in such a situation can be tricky because it is not easy to apply enough nitrogen to feed the plants and supply the bacteria, yet at the same time not burn the plants.

Since nitrogen is very volatile, it easily escapes into the air. Aged manure and compost, although wonderful as humus, seldom contain enough nitrogen to supply all the needs of a plant, so additional fertilizer is nearly always required for daylilies and other heavy feeders. Organic gardeners use cottonseed meal, seaweed, alfalfa pellets, soybean meal, dried blood, or composted sewage such as Milorganite as sources of supplemental nitrogen. Those who prefer chemical fertilizers add 5-10-10 at the rate of 2 or 3 pounds per 100 square feet. When preparing the soil, mix the fertilizer and organic matter thoroughly into the soil so the plants won't need to search for nutrients.

When you add fertilizer to the soil, play it safe and use only moderate amounts. You can add more nutrients after the plants begin to grow, if you find you guessed on the short side originally. Too little fertilizer is not healthy for daylilies, but too much can be even worse. Chemical fertilizers in excessive amounts can burn plants and may even kill them, but even if you use organic plant food or one of the "safe" slow-acting chemical types, don't be overgenerous. Daylilies growing in soil that is too rich are likely to

develop lush foliage, but few blossoms.

If you are having trouble growing plants, chemical tests of the soil may help you identify the reasons. Extension services and garden stores can often do these for you, or you can test your own with a soil testing kit available from most garden and farm stores. Tests for phosphorus and potassium can indicate too much or too little of either element, but nitrogen is so volatile that, unless the soil has been recently fertilized, a test nearly always tells you that more is needed. A soil test kit is not difficult to use, although a few minutes are needed for the soil-chemical solution to change color.

Compost — Homemade, Free Fertilizer

In our opinion, no gardener should be without a compost pile. It not only provides the nutrient-rich humus that daylilies love, but also helps to recycle garden wastes, lawn clippings, leaves, and garbage. Humus allows the soil to retain moisture and store nutrients for later use; and it buffers the soil against excessive acidity or alkalinity.

Many organic gardeners take compost making very seriously. They buy elaborate kits, shred raw materials, turn their piles frequently, and add activators, earthworms, and other things to speed up the process. If you have a limited amount of space and need only a small amount of compost, these techniques are practical. On the other hand, if you use a lot of compost, have room for more than one pile, and are not able to spend time fussing with your pile, you can get good results without all that effort and expense.

We are rather casual about our own compost making and expend a minimum of effort, but it works. Two piles are always in process near our garden — one being made and the other being used. We spread alternate layers of green matter from the garden, clippings, leaves, and garbage with layers of soil and manure, and the earthworms find it by themselves. We do not turn the pile but try to keep it flat so the rain will soak in and it will remain damp. If the weather is dry, we water it with a hose.

Friends of ours use only one tall pile. They keep adding layers to the top, and shovel out what they need from the bottom. The decomposition takes place as everything settles, and by the time it hits the bottom, it is ready for use.

It takes about a year for the organic materials to decompose if you don't do anything to speed up the decomposition. If you add activators and turn the pile frequently, it may take only a few months.

Soil pH and Trace Elements

Daylilies grow in a wide range of acidic and alkaline conditions, but they seem to prefer a pH of between 5.5 and 7, with 6 to 6.5 being ideal. This pH is about the same as most garden plants prefer, but it is less acidic than that recommended for primula, potatoes, and strawberries. We test regularly for

pH, using either an inexpensive chemical kit or an electronic instrument that shows the results immediately. We like both but feel that the chemical test is more accurate. Many times you can guess the pH of the soil near the surface by observing the weeds that are growing. Clover and goldenrod indicate an alkaline soil, for example, but sorrel is a sign of acidic soil.

It may be necessary to test the soil for pH every few years if the subsoil in your region is naturally very acidic or alkaline. Where we live the subsoil is loaded with lime, and every hard rain tends to make it percolate upward into our topsoil. It creates an excellent medium for daylilies but keeps us from successfully raising blueberries, azaleas, or other acid-loving plants.

If you need to raise the soil pH, dolomitic limestone is recommended because daylilies thrive with magnesium. If your soil already tests at 6.5 or above, do not use additional lime, but when you add fertilizer, use one that contains magnesium, such as a 5-10-10-2 formula (5 percent nitrogen, 10 percent phosphorus, 10 percent potassium, and 2 percent magnesium). If that is not available or you prefer not to use a chemical plant food, mix a small amount of Epsom salts with water and pour it over the plants.

Lime tends to move through the soil slowly, so for best results mix it thoroughly into the soil whether you are adding it before planting or spreading it around established plants.

Daylilies in Raised Beds?

Many gardeners like to plant daylilies in beds that are raised anywhere from a few inches to a foot or more above the lawn or surrounding paths. Raised beds have many decided advantages: they are easier to weed and care for without bending as much as you'd need to in a conventional planting; the extra soil depth allows more space for healthy root growth; and if the land is wet, the height allows for better drainage. Although all instructions for raising daylilies stress their need for moisture during the growing season, they do not grow well in swampy soil. Raised beds also warm up faster than the surrounding earth, so the plants start to grow earlier in the spring and

Raised beds are easier to weed, the extra soil depth allows more space for healthy root growth, and, in wet areas they provide better drainage.

therefore blossom a bit earlier, which is often good in northern gardens.

Raised beds are an obvious advantage when there is danger that heavy rains might flood the beds for several days at a time, or that ice will form there during the cold months. The elevation of a raised bed can help prevent both problems. Although snow is a good insulator against winter's cold, ice is not.

Unfortunately, raised beds dry out much faster than those that are on the level, and even when they are mulched they require more waterings in a dry season. If your soil is sandy or if you garden where summers tend to be dry and short of rainfall, it is best to avoid raised beds and plant your daylilies in a conventional bed.

If you decide to plant in a raised bed, treated landscape timbers or old railroad ties work well to hold the soil in place. Use the ties only if the toxic creosote applied as a preservative has leached away over the years; otherwise, it is best not to use them near plants.

Edgings

Although daylilies are good self-edgers because it is possible to mow up to the foliage, an edging of some sort nevertheless provides a handsome finishing touch to a border or mass planting. It also keeps the lawn grasses from creeping into the bed. Some types can be added after the plants are in the ground, but others should be installed before any planting.

The edging requiring the least care is not, strictly speaking, an edging at all but a pathway constructed between the daylilies and the lawn. Crushed rock, gravel, flagstone, brick, concrete, wooden timbers, asphalt, or any similar material makes an attractive surface and separates grass from the plants.

Steel, plastic, or aluminum edgings also make useful barriers between the lawn and a flower bed. They come in rolls 4 inches or more in width and are inserted vertically into the soil in a ditch cut at the edge of the bed, so that the top of the edging is at ground level. This type is effective if it is wide enough and set properly, but if it is set too high, it can be unsightly and may catch the lawnmower. If it is set too low or sinks into the ground, its usefulness disappears, since grasses creep over it and into the bed. Some lawn grasses are shallow rooted, and a 4-inch width is adequate for them; but lawns nearly always contain a few weedy grasses such as quackgrass, and their roots reach much deeper, necessitating at least an 8-inch barrier.

Edgings are sometimes made the feature of a garden rather than being hidden away and made inconspicuous. A row of partially buried bricks stood on end, either vertically or at a slant, makes an appealing border. Landscape timbers of wood or plastic, round fence rails, or paving blocks set on edge are other possibilities. We have even seen 4-inch round sewer pipe painted brown used as edging; you'd never have guessed its original purpose.

The simplest kind of edging is a ditch cut into the soil between the lawn and the flowers. It can be dug with a spade or a manual edging tool made specifically for

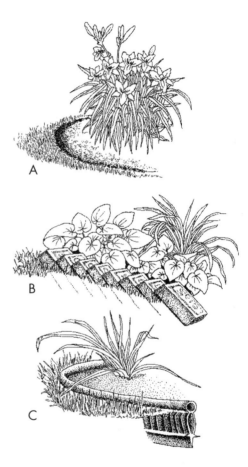

An edging provides a handsome finishing touch to a flower border. The simplest edging is (A) a ditch cut into the soil between the lawn and the flowers; (B) bricks, laid at an angle for better drainage, are so attractive that they become a design feature; (C) plastic edging acts as an excellent weed barrier and lasts indefinitely.

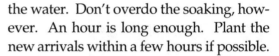

this job; for a large area, electric- and gasoline-powered edgers are available. Although a ditch-type edging looks nice, it is necessary to recut it frequently throughout the summer if it is to retain its neat appearance.

Handling New Plants

Once the soil has been well prepared, now comes the fun of actually planting your new daylilies. When you have ordered them by mail, you usually receive large, healthy plants. They may look more like old dead roots than healthy plants when you unpack them, but don't be discouraged. Nurseries do not pack daylilies in moist packing for mailing as they would strawberry plants, because daylily roots and crowns are likely to rot if they remain moist for long periods.

As soon as you open the package, pour water over the plants, or, better yet, unpack them and soak the roots for an hour or so in water that is cool, but not cold. If you have liquid fertilizer on hand, add a tiny bit to the water. Don't overdo the soaking, however. An hour is long enough. Plant the new arrivals within a few hours if possible.

If the bed is not yet ready the day the plants come, heel them in (see illustration) temporarily in a vacant spot in the vegetable garden or in a cold frame. Water them thoroughly right after you plant them, again using a weak solution of liquid fertilizer. This treatment will help them recover from the shock of being dug, packed, and shipped.

If you have been lucky enough to get good-sized plants, you may be tempted to split them into two or three divisions so you can have a garden full of blooms more quickly. It is best to resist the urge. A large plant will recover much faster than a small one from the shock of being uprooted and moved many miles; it will give you more and larger flowers faster than several small, frail plants, which are likely to take an extra year or two to recover and reach maturity.

Some growers like to pamper their new daylilies by putting them into pots for a few weeks to get them off to a faster start. We pot the ones that seem a bit weak, especially when they are in the high-priced class, so we can be sure that they get special attention. If you decide to take this step as extra insurance, use some of your best soil in the pot — either commercial potting soil, an

To "heel in" plants that you are unable to plant immediately, dig a shallow trench, lay the plants on their sides with their roots in the trench, and cover the roots lightly with soil; do not let the soil dry out.

artificial soil mix, or good garden soil mixed with a little sand and peat. Keep the plant watered, and once a week feed it a weak solution of liquid fertilizer. For the first few days keep it out of the midday sun, too.

Some northern gardeners, when they get daylilies from the deep South or from California, cut all the plants' roots back to about an inch below the crown before planting them. They reason that the old roots will never adapt properly to the cooler northern soils and severe winters, but if the plant is forced to grow a batch of new roots, the new ones will be more hardy. Though some growers swear by this practice, we have never tried it so we do not know from firsthand experience how well it works. If you try it, we recommend that you pot up the plant and pamper it for the first few weeks, as we suggested previously, to help compensate for the surgery.

Spacing the Plants

The most common mistake most of us make when planting is to set everything too close together. Although proximity of plants means that there is less room for weeds and less land is used, some daylilies increase in size very rapidly. Crowded plants not only look unsightly and don't bloom well, but good air circulation around the plants that helps prevent disease is inhibited.

Set most plants at least 2 feet apart from each other or other plants; provide the vigorous kinds with at least a 3-foot spacing;

and set miniatures from 15 to 18 inches apart. Since new plants are small, they are sure to look lonely the first year. If all that space bothers you, plant a few annuals or geraniums among the new daylilies to fill in the spaces and furnish color. Be patient. Daylily blooms do not look their best until at least the second year after planting, and the less vigorous kinds may take longer to form sizable clumps.

The most effective way to group daylilies if they are not in a mass planting is to plant them in clumps of the same cultivar. This is particularly true in a garden border where they are interspersed with other perennials. One large daylily is enough to form a nice clump in a small or medium-sized garden, but in a large border, a grouping of at least three plants of the same cultivar is more effective. When you are using miniatures, three to five of the same cultivar make a good clump.

Setting the Plants

A trowel is a good tool for setting small plants in a bed, but if you have been lucky enough to acquire large clumps, you will need a spade to dig the holes. Unless it has already rained substantially that day, we always fill the holes with water before planting the daylilies. We then add enough soil to fill the bottom of the holes so we can set the plants at the proper depth. The crown — the area where the root clump meets the foliage — should be level with

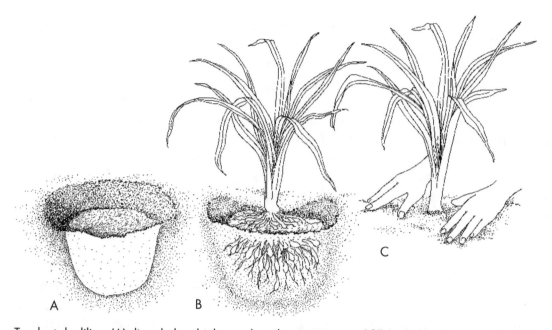

To plant daylilies, (A) dig a hole a bit larger than the root area and fill the hole with water; (B) add enough enriched soil to the bottom of the hole so you can set the plants at the proper depth; (C) add soil all around the plant, being sure to keep the crown exactly level with the top of the ground, and press the soil firmly in place. Keep the plant well watered for the week or two after planting.

the top of the ground (see illustration). Plants set too deep tend to grow poorly, clump up slowly, and not bloom well. If they are set too high, the roots will be exposed and will dry out easily, which, of course, is not good for the health of the plant.

Although it is best to set the plants into loose, humus-rich soil so the roots will begin to grow rapidly, it is equally important, for two reasons, to press the soil firmly around each plant after you have set it. First, you want to squeeze out any pockets of air that might be trapped there and would be likely to dry out the roots. Second, when the soil is too loose, daylilies tend to sink

deeper into the earth, often so low that the crown becomes buried; the effect is the same as if the plant had been set too deep. We recommend occasionally checking all the newly set plants throughout the first year to make sure they have not sunk. If they have, dig them up and reset them.

Although daylilies are about as undemanding as any perennials could be, they still require water, especially directly after they are planted, when their roots do not yet reach far down to find moisture in the soil. Many of the poor-looking beds we have seen were the result of a dry season in which their caretakers neglected to water the plants. Watering is one of the best things you can do for a new cultivar, and without it you can lose a valuable plant; or, if it survives, it loses an entire season's growth.

Water the plants every other day for a week or two after you have set them in the ground, unless it rains heavily. Then water them once a week thereafter until you are sure they are well established. When you plant in spring or summer, add some liquid fertilizer such as fish emulsion or liquid seaweed to the water once a week; or, if you have manure available, mix a shovelful into a bucket of water, stir it furiously, and water with the manure "tea." If you prefer chemicals, use Peters, Rapid-gro, Miracle-Gro, or a similar product, and follow the mixing directions on the package. Continue to add liquid fertilizer each week for a month. The plants will get off to a good start and grow rapidly during the long days of early summer and will be well established before winter sets in.

Even after daylilies have become well established, water them whenever there isn't enough rain, especially during the budding and blooming seasons. Avoid light sprinklings, because the water never reaches far enough down to help the thirsty roots, especially if it has to pass through a heavy mulch that absorbs the moisture. A good soaking every three or four days is preferable to a light sprinkle every day. Use fertilizers more sparingly after the first season so that you do not encourage too much leaf growth at the

expense of blooms (see Chapter 7).

Even with fall planting, watering is necessary to prevent the roots from drying out and to help the plants get established for their spring growth.

Mulches

The advantages of using mulches have been stressed so much in recent years that we won't dwell on them. An organic mulch protects the soil against erosion, checks weed growth, adds fertility and humus to the soil, and helps keep the temperature of the soil constant. A mulch is particularly important to daylilies because even more than many other plants, they need, as we've said, a great deal of moisture during their growing and blooming seasons. Mulches not only trap the moisture from melting snows in the spring, but they also allow hard summer rains to be stored long enough to be used before they evaporate.

Because we were aware of daylilies' need for water, especially in the blossoming season, we were pleasantly surprised at a discovery forced upon us one exceptionally hot, dry July when an unexpected visit to the hospital caused us to neglect the beds for three weeks. We were amazed that all the plants survived without being watered even during the height of bloom. The flowers were not as large or as prolific as they would have been if they had received all the moisture they needed, but the mulch apparently protected the small amount of moisture in the ground, and that was enough to keep the plants alive and blooming. It taught us to never neglect the annual mulching.

Many organic materials are suitable as mulch, so search for whatever is attractive and readily available in your area. We use shredded bark from a local mill; other nearby gardeners use wood chips or shavings, leaves, lawn clippings, ground-up corn

Daylilies respond particularly well to mulching because of their need for plenty of moisture during their growing and blooming seasons. If you apply mulch more than 1 inch deep, be sure to leave a bit of open space around each plant.

cobs, old silage, or hay. In addition to these materials, gardeners in other locations use salt hay, cocoa hulls, citrus pulp, or other commercial mulches. Sawdust is not a good mulch because it packs too hard and robs nitrogen from the soil. It isn't a good idea either to spread permanent mulches such as crushed rock, marble chips, or flagstones which might be used around evergreens or flowering shrubs, because you'll need to dig and divide your daylilies from time to time, and you may also want to move them about occasionally. It is difficult not to disturb nonorganic mulches during these operations.

There are a few precautions to take when you use mulch around daylilies. If you apply a depth of more than an inch, do not pile it directly against the daylily foliage but instead, leave a bit of open space around each plant. Otherwise, the mulch may smother the crown and the effect would be the same as if you had buried it too deep.

Mulches aren't perfect, in spite of our raves about them. Although they prevent evaporation of moisture that is already in the soil, in a dry season they also soak up any light showers and prevent the water from trickling deep enough into the soil to reach the plant's roots. In the same way, they also absorb light waterings. Peat moss, particularly, is not a good mulch because of its absorbent qualities, and also because, when it is dry, it tends to blow away.

An organic mulch can also tie up some of the fertility in the soil the first year that it is applied. Mulch decomposes from the bottom where it touches the soil, and, as we have said, the bacteria need nitrogen for this process. The liquid fertilizer that you will be using the first summer should compensate for this, however, and as you add new mulch each year, the old mulch that has already decomposed will furnish sufficient nutrients for both the bacteria and the plants.

Giving your long-lived daylilies a bit of extra care at planting time not only rewards you with more and better flowers earlier, but also assures that less effort will be needed to keep the bed weed free. A few hours spent in planning the garden and getting the soil in good condition will save you dozens of hours of work over the years — time you can in good conscience allot to enjoying your extraordinary daylilies.

Labeling

We strongly believe in labeling daylilies as soon as they are planted. Of course, with a nursery we don't have any choice, but we would do it anyway because of our poor memories. There are many reasons for labels. If you accidentally lose a choice daylily, you will certainly want to replace it. Also, when visitors admire your plants, they are sure to inquire: "What's the name of that lovely ruffled daylily?" And when you give away a plant, it doubles in value in the recipient's estimation if the genuine name is attached.

Garden centers and seed catalogs offer many different types of plant labels, and you may want to experiment with several kinds before deciding which are best for you. You may even choose to make your own out of some material that fits well into your landscaping.

Daylilies, unlike woody shrubs or trees, cannot have a label attached to the plant. It should be placed close to the plant yet still not interfere with its growth. In a home garden it should also be as permanent and inconspicuous as possible. Some mail-order nurseries mark their plants with labels that can be used in the garden, but most soon fade and need replacing. Wooden stakes, either plain or painted white, are most common and usually the least expensive. When you mark the painted ones with a nursery marking pen (see Appendix) or soft lead pencil, they usually last a couple of years, and even longer if you spray them with a clear lacquer after marking.

Our favorite permanent labels are the aluminum tags that can be marked with a ballpoint pen or pencil which embosses the plant name into the tag. The tags come with short aluminum wires attached, and you can fasten them to small, aluminum or bamboo stakes, but we prefer to recycle used, ½-inch, black plastic pipe which we cut into foot-long pieces with hand pruners; then we cut a hole, with a jacknife or punch, in what will be the top end, and fasten on the label wires. We hammer these into the earth near the plant. They are inconspicuous, and although they cannot be read unless you bend over, they are always there when you need them. We have used this type for many years, and the original ones are still easy to read.

Zinc labels on galvanized metal legs are popular with some growers. They are approximately 1″ x 2½″ in size, stand 10 inches high, and when marked with a permanent-type marker, are very durable.

Although most homeowners would not want large, white plastic labels cluttering up their backyard border, we use them to mark our display beds, so visitors can easily identify the different cultivars. Although we take them indoors for the winter, they are unable to withstand more than two or three seasons before they become yellowed and brittle.

We have a friend who uses small, green plastic labels in his daylily garden. They are carefully placed, so most visitors would never notice them, but he can spot them easily and reel off the names of his hundreds of plants in a knowledgeable way. The green plastic labels appear to last longer than the white ones, but we have been unable to find a pen or other marker to use on them that does not fade in a season or two.

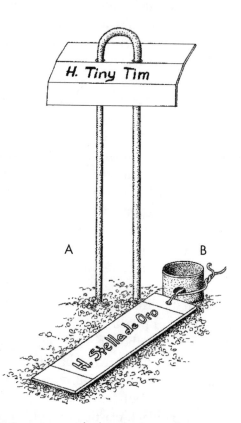

Aluminum tags make long-lasting permanent labels for your plants. Some are available with (A) a U-shaped wire stake that slips easily into the soil; or (B) you can use tags that come with short wires attached and fasten them to ½-inch, black plastic pipe that has been cut into foot-long pieces and hammered into the earth near the plant. Some gardeners cut up old aluminum pie plates to use as labels.

Reviving an Old Daylily Bed

At some point you may need to remake a long-neglected daylily bed, or perhaps you have recently acquired a home with one that fits that description. With a bit of hard work you will no doubt be able to turn the weedy old eyesore into a beautiful garden, because daylilies can survive years of inattention better than most other perennials.

Look over the bed carefully and decide at the outset what kind of planting you eventually would like in that spot. If you decide you simply want a bed of flowers rather than the latest, biggest, and best day-lily cultivars, you can probably use many of the plants that are in the garden already. If the old bed is completely overgrown, the daylilies that have survived are likely to be the tough, rather uninteresting kinds, and it is likely that few of them are worth using in a flower garden, since there are so many better cultivars now available.

If you have the space, the easiest procedure is to dig a new bed in another spot and move the plants you decide to keep, rather than attempt to remake the existing bed. That way, week by week, as the plants in the old bed bloom, you can select the ones you like and move them to their new quarters. By moving them when they are in bloom (see Chapter 9), you will be able to arrange them according to heights and blooming times. Strictly speaking, of course, you would then be making a new bed rather than revitalizing the old one.

If you choose to revive the old bed exactly where it is, the most efficient way to do it is to dig out all the plants on a cloudy day in late spring after everything has started to grow and you are able to tell which are daylilies and which are weeds. Place them on a large sheet of plastic to keep the lawn clean. Since the procedure will take time, cover them with an old sheet and sprinkle them occasionally, so they won't dry out. Then redig, fertilize, and thoroughly cultivate the bed before resetting the plants you choose to keep. Work as fast as you can — or bribe a kid to help — so that the plants you have dug can get their roots back into the earth as soon as possible. Chances are that most of the clumps in an old bed will be very large. Before you replant, you can split each of them into several smaller plants with quick thrusts of a sharp, rounded spade. Treating them roughly shouldn't hurt the old vigorous types a bit. You may want to add to the bed some newer daylily cultivars, so leave some spaces for them, even if it means throwing away some of your heap.

One problem in remaking an old bed is that you may have trouble getting rid of all the old-timers that have been growing there for decades. Many of the species and their varieties are stoloniferous, which means that new plants grow easily from the root tips, like quackgrass, and it is almost impossible to dig out every root.

C H A P T E R 7

Daylily Culture

HOEING THE VEGETABLE GARDEN is work, mowing the lawn is work, and raking autumn leaves is work. But somehow the things we do to help our daylilies grow don't seem like work, any more than we consider feeding the birds or taking care of Dudley, our cat, to be in that category. When you enjoy something as much as we enjoy daylilies, it's a pleasure to look after them. The daylilies reward us handsomely for every bit of attention we give them, and they ask for very little. In fact, we know of plants that have suffered because loving gardeners gave them too much attention and showered them with excesses of fertilizer, lime, mulch, and water. Even the little care that daylilies need will be less if you prepared the soil well before you planted them, spaced the plants far enough apart, and fed and watered them the first year so they would get off to a fast healthy start (see Chapter 6).

Before we describe the few seasonal things you can do that will help your day-lilies thrive, let's briefly talk about the three basics: feeding, watering, and weeding.

Food for Thought — and Growth

After a plant has grown a year and appears to be well established, if it looks good and is blooming well, don't give it more fertilizer. Instead, simply add to the mulch. Blooms are what you are after, and if the plant is growing too vigorously, it will concentrate on producing an overabundance of leaves and roots rather than flowers. Also, if it grows too fast, the clump will need dividing sooner to keep it healthy. If it looks tired and is not producing new fans, however, give it a small amount of plant food.

It is easy to become confused if you listen to all the fertilizing suggestions experts give for daylilies because each seems convinced that his or her particular feeding program is the secret of growing success. Organic gardeners maintain that only natural fertilizers should get near the roots of any plant. They suggest bone meal, blood meal, kelp, fish emulsion, greensand, manures of all kinds, compost, and seaweed, as well as commercially packaged natural plant foods. Other growers swear by the results they get from using chemical fertilizers, such as granulated 5-10-10 or liquid products like Miracle-Gro. Some use only slow-acting products like Osmocote. Still others declare they never use fertilizer at all but depend only on an organic mulch that slowly composts on top of the soil, and on the abundant earthworm populations the mulch encourages. This natural treatment, they feel, furnishes all the nutrients that daylilies really need.

So, you "pays yer money and you takes yer choice," as the old-time country fair barkers used to say. No one fertilizing method has been proven the "correct" one for feeding daylilies, but like every other living thing, they need nourishment, and the poorer the soil conditions, the more care you should take to see that they get it. We prefer natural fertilizers not only because they are safer to use, but also because they provide for a daylily's needs over a long period of time, unlike chemical plant foods, which supply a heavy dose of nutrients that the plant may absorb immediately whether it needs them or not.

Daylilies Need Plenty of Water

We rarely need to water our established daylilies because our New England summers are cool and short, and the climate usually provides enough rainfall. Gardeners who live in warmer and drier parts of the country, however, need to provide what nature does not. A great deal of moisture is necessary for daylily plants to produce a crop of new flowers each day during the blooming season, and it is likely that gardeners who complain about their meager crop of poor flowers have neglected to water them enough.

A garden hose works well for watering, but it is time-consuming if you have a large number of daylilies. With a hose you must be careful that the force of the water does not wash out newly set plants or knock off buds or blooms. Sprinklers on stakes are a good solution for providing water, but because drops of water falling directly on many types of red and orange daylily blossoms produce light-colored water blotches on the petals, many gardeners prefer to use soaker hoses or trickle irrigation.

Since water moves through the soil very slowly, light sprinklings or short, hard showers on a hot summer day usually evaporate before the moisture has a chance to sink deep enough into the soil to help the plants. When you supply water, do it gently enough so it won't run off, and for long enough periods to enable it to soak deeply into the soil. Otherwise you'll probably be wasting both water and time.

Plant authorities used to warn gardeners never to water in the evening because the additional humidity would promote disease. Like many old-time warnings, however, this one seems to have been discontinued. Common sense tells us that heavy dew comes in the evening, as do many summer showers, and both beautifully refresh the plants. We always try to water our daylilies in the evening because the moisture is less likely to evaporate quickly then, and more of it soaks down to the roots of the plants where it will do the most good. Also, when we use a hose or an overhead sprinkler, there is less chance of damaging or blotching the flowers, because most of the blooms are due to close in a short time, and a fresh unscathed batch will appear the following morning.

Weed Control in the Daylily Bed

We don't find pulling weeds as much fun as other aspects of garden care, although some of our friends who work away from home claim that a weekend of yanking out the villains is healthy, therapeutic exercise after a hard week of working at an indoor job.

Most daylilies, with the exception of the older, tough species, need some protection from the weeds that commandeer their moisture and nutrients. Weeds also compete for space, crowd the daylilies and leave them less room to grow. When certain weed species, like goldenrod, become tall enough, they even deprive them of sunlight.

Prevention is the ideal way to cope. Far fewer unwanted weeds appear in a garden in which the soil has been carefully prepared and all weeds removed before planting. The sprouting of new ones can be eliminated to a great extent by the use of a mulch be-

tween the plants, which smothers the sprouting weeds. Much of the weed problem in country gardens comes from nearby dandelions, goldenrod, milkweed, and thistles that spread their wind-blown seeds into the bed. A mulch helps to prevent these seeds from touching the soil and sprouting, because they dry out first.

Other preventative measures include getting rid of nearby weeds that produce fuzzy, airborne seeds. Use only manure and compost that are completely decomposed, because if they are partially decomposed they always contain an abundance of healthy weed seeds which can wreak havoc on a garden. Using weed-free materials such as mulch also reduces volunteer plant life. As we have said, the weeds that proliferate by underground stolons, such as quack grass (we call it witchgrass, and our Canadian friends call it twichgrass), can be kept outside the garden by using a vertically installed edging of steel, aluminum, or heavy plastic around the daylily bed.

The weeds that actually push through a mulch are shallow-rooted and easy to pull, so in a small garden it is fairly simple to keep them under control. By yanking them out early when they are young, before they have a chance to reproduce, you'll save a lot of work later. Pulling weeds by hand does less damage to the roots of adjoining daylilies and other plants than using a hoe, cultivator, or hand-held power tiller. Hand-weeding is not only much safer than the use of chemicals, but it is also cheaper. You need only a few minutes each day or an hour or so each week to keep a fair-sized garden tidy.

Weedkillers

We do not recommend using any herbicides on the home garden unless you cannot cope in any other way. If you decide to use an herbicide, read all the directions that come with the package before you buy it to find out what types of weeds are controlled by the product, which plants it can be used on safely, and what, if any, precautions you should take. Follow the directions exactly, for your own safety, the safety of the plants, and the safety of the environment.

Results of the application of any herbicide vary greatly according to rainfall, temperature, soil type, the stage of growth the plant is in at the time of treatment, and other factors. The uncertainty of the results, in addition to the expense of the products, and the feeling that chemicals should not be sprayed on the soil, makes other types of weed control much more acceptable to most home gardeners.

Most people with large flower borders, exhibition gardens, and nurseries, however, can no longer rely, as they once did, on a staff of skilled gardeners to keep their landscape neat. Finding anyone willing to pull weeds for hours is not an easy task, and the expense can be prohibitive. Such growers often resort to herbicides to keep their plantings presentable.

The early herbicides have been proven to be dangerous to the environment, pets, and people, and fortunately they have been taken off the market or restricted to professionals; present-day gardeners now have a variety of products that have been more thoroughly tested, some of which are even endorsed by organic gardeners.

Daylilies are remarkably resistant to many of the commonly used herbicides, and when they are used at the recommended rates, they eliminate the weeds but do not damage the plants. Like most nurseries, we occasionally find it necessary to use some of those that are rated as safe in order to keep our plantings weed free and presentable to the public; but of course we avoid the use of any chemical, even the so-called "natural" ones, on daylilies from which we plan to eat any of the buds.

The list of recommended herbicides keeps changing as new ones come on the market, and it also varies among different states, so we do not suggest specific names. If you feel you must use chemicals for weed control, ask your local garden center or farm store for up-to-date advice, or consult your agricultural agent.

Herbicides work in several ways. Those called preemergents are probably the most useful. They prevent the sprouting of seeds that have blown into the daylily bed or are brought in with fresh manure, hay mulch, or unfinished compost. When they are used according to directions, they do not harm plants that are already established. Some types can be sprinkled over the soil around newly set daylilies at planting time, but it is safer to wait a full growing season until after the plants have become well established, before using them. Most preemergents must be incorporated into the soil immediately after application either by cultivation, heavy rains, or irrigation. If not, their ability to control weeds will be lost by exposure to the air and sunlight. Do not expect preemergents to control the germination of every type of weed. They do a good job but there are always exceptions. The length of time that they remain active in the soil varies greatly, too. Because few prevent the sprouting of weeds for an entire season, it may be necessary to apply additional treatments, especially during the late summer, when many weeds scatter their seeds.

Another group of herbicides kill existing weeds by absorption either through their roots or foliage. Those that work through the foliage are meant to be sprayed over the weeds when they are actively growing. Those that act on roots are applied by mixing a soluble form with water and sprinkling it over the soil, or by spreading a granular form on the surface of the soil, usually when the plants are dormant. Most of these types of herbicides are highly selective: some control only certain broadleaf weeds, and others kill only grasses. Although a few kinds kill all types of vegetation, they are not recommended for home gardeners.

Springtime in the Daylily Bed

The care you gave your daylilies when you planted them begins to pay off the following spring when the fresh new shoots poke through the earth and the healthy clumps of greenery begin to expand.

Early spring is the time to remove any protective winter coverings you might have placed over the plants the previous fall. Wait until all danger of ground-freezing weather is over, however, before uncovering the plants, because the new sprouts that start early will be tender. Check to be sure the mulch around the plants is not covering the crowns; and inspect all your young plants to make sure the crowns haven't sunk into the ground over the winter, or that frost has not heaved the plants out so the roots will dry in the sun. Reset any that need it to the proper depth, and firm the earth around them.

If your garden has been under snow all winter, you may find that the neighborhood moles have been active even when the chipmunks and woodchucks were sleeping. Mole tunnels not only allow air to flow around the roots, but they also permit mice to enter and feed on the nutritious, tasty morsels. Move some soil to fill in any mole burrows. Spreading a few mothballs in the burrows sometimes stimulates the creatures to move out of your planting area, although forcing them to suddenly change their residence may not help your friendly relationship with the neighbors.

Other than the spring sickness described in Chapter 8, daylilies have few diseases or insects that bother them in the spring. If you notice anything unusual, however, take action right away, before the trouble spreads.

Spring is a good time to divide any clumps that are getting too large, and to split up any cultivars you want to use to get more plants (see directions, pages 97-98). When a clump becomes too large, not only are its health and blooming ability affected, but it may also crowd neighboring daylilies or other plants. You can tell when a clump has reached this stage because the flowers become smaller and fewer, and sometimes you'll see dead fans forming in the center of the clump.

Fortunately, daylilies don't need to be divided every year like iris and chrysanthemums. Vigorous kinds may need to be split up every five to seven years, but the less lively cultivars may need this treatment only every ten years or so. A large clump can be split into a half-dozen or more good-sized smaller clumps; and the less vigorous cultivars, into two or three.

Pull out any weeds that are pushing their way up through the mulch. Annual weeds will be sprouting, and if the ground isn't frozen, perennial weeds such as quack grass grow throughout much of the winter unless you have successfully barred them from the bed.

Spring is the time to add fertilizer to the soil around the plants if they appear to need it, and to replenish the mulch, if you didn't do that chore the previous fall. Mulched plants develop roots that are more shallow than those of unmulched plants, so if the mulch is not replenished annually, the roots could dry out and the plant would suffer.

For us, spring is when we "houseclean" away the old dead foliage from the plants. Although some gardeners do it in the fall, especially in warmer climates, it is a chore we seldom find time to accomplish before snow buries our daylilies; and anyway, we rationalize, it acts as additional mulch. The foliage and scapes are easier to remove in the spring because they have deteriorated, and much of the cleanup can be done with a rake, although we usually need to pull away some stalks by hand. The primary reason for cleaning it away is for appearance, and on our mass plantings we usually leave it because it makes a good mulch. None of it is wasted, however, because whatever we take off makes a good addition to the compost pile.

Summer — Well Worth Waiting For

Summer is the time to relax and enjoy the beautiful blooms, so "don't forget to smell the flowers." They won't be there tomorrow.

Don't be disappointed if the daylilies you planted in the spring, or even the year before, are not loaded with breathtaking blooms. The plants should last a lifetime, and you can't expect them to put on a great display immediately, especially if you started with small plants. Because it takes time for a good clump of fans and scapes to develop, anyone who demands a garden overflowing with blooms the first summer had better stick with geraniums.

Once you have a collection of daylilies, you will notice that some are very neat, and their faded blooms shrivel up so well that you can hardly see their inconspicuous remains the day after they fade. They usually fall off within two or three days. Others, especially double cultivars and those with gorgeous large flowers that have heavy petal substance and ruffles, conspicuously hang on the scapes for several days, making the clump look messy and unkempt.

If you have hundreds of plants, you can hardly keep thousands of faded flowers removed every day, but if your patch is small or you have special clumps that are always seen closeup, you may want to make "deadheading" a regular morning event. Sometimes we carry small pails attached to our belts for picking off the dead blooms in our border plantings and those around the entrance to our home; but in the nursery, the task is so major that grooming is gener-ally left undone.

Because catalog descriptions seldom mention whether or not a cultivar is self-grooming, it is difficult to find out in ad-vance how long a particular plant holds its faded blooms, and whether it will require this additional chore. Since most of the plants that have this lingering habit are real beauties, we feel it is worthwhile to put up with the nuisance. Someday dedicated breeders may decide to concentrate on de-veloping plants with good grooming habits.

Even if faded blooms are not a prob-lem in your beds, keep an eye out for the seedpods that sometimes form after the flowers have disappeared. Some variet-ies produce large numbers of pods, either because they are good mother plants, or simply because their pistil is short enough so bees can easily dust it with pollen as they enter and leave the flower.

Developing several pods full of seeds takes a great deal of energy from a plant, which is seldom a major problem with the older varieties that have vim and vigor to spare, but it can weaken less energetic hybrids and result in poor growth and reduced flowering in the following years. Unless you are hybridizing and planning to save the seeds, pick off any tiny pods as soon as you see them. They are easy to distinguish from the developing flower buds.

Although overproduction of blooms is seldom a problem with older, estab-lished daylily clumps, young plants that bloom very heavily, especially those that

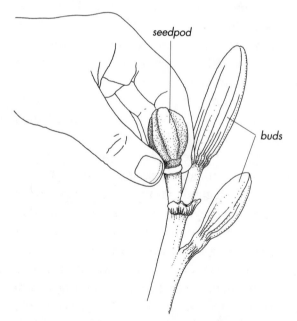

seedpod

buds

Unless you are planning to save seeds, pick off any developing seedpods as soon as you see them; seed production tends to weaken less energetic hybrids and results in poor growth and reduced flowering in subsequent years.

bloom over a long season, may become weakened by overproduction just as fruit trees sometimes suffer from overbearing. If a plant appears too small and frail to support the large number of buds forming on its scapes, either cut off part of the scapes or simply pick off a few of the buds. The remaining flowers will be larger, even though there are fewer of them, and the plant can put its energy into making new growth for future years. No one likes to nip a flower in the bud, but there are times when it is a kindness to the plant to do so.

Occasionally, if there has been a lot of rain and the plants have been overfertilized, an otherwise well-behaved daylily may grow a huge mass of tall, dense foliage. When this happens, the leaves sometimes partially hide the blooms. A careful haircut with a pair of grass shears is all that is needed to show off the flowers.

The brown that appears on the foliage of some cultivars in mid-to-late summer is disheartening, especially since it often appears during the heaviest blooming period. The condition is not the same as spring sickness, or the so-called "yellows" (see Chapter 8), and no one is certain what causes the disfiguration. Extremes in weather and other stressful conditions, such as too much or too little fertilizer or lime, seem to make it worse some years than others. The malady doesn't appear to spread from plant to plant, and unless the condition is unusually bad, the plant's long-term health isn't greatly affected. Different kinds of viruses have been discovered in daylilies from time to time,

but none of these has yet been proven as a contributing factor to the distressing "browns."

Summer is a good time to examine the plants carefully to see which should be moved to a more appropriate spot and which, if any, should be discarded and replaced by new ones with better blooming habits. We prefer to move daylilies when they are dormant, but since we can't distinguish colors and heights at that time, we take notes or mark the plants when they are in bloom. In our garden notebook we might write that the color of 'Chicago Rosy' isn't compatible with 'Bright Banner', or that a new 'Hyperion' should be moved to the empty spot where a weak new cultivar is barely hanging on; or we remind ourselves that the tall 'Challenger' must be moved to the back of the border.

When immediate action seems the best route, you can safely move daylilies even when they are blooming if you include a large clump of earth with the plant. Choose a rainy or cloudy day, or if that is not possible, move it on a cool evening to minimize the shock to the plant. Water it each day thereafter for several days, as survival insurance, and if the daylily still complains by wilting, place a large cardboard carton, garbage can, or paper bag over the entire plant to protect it from the sun and drying breezes for a few days.

Keep an eye out through the summer for any insects or diseases on the plants, but do not panic if you notice a few bugs around them. Daylilies are remarkably pest resistant, and often this factor plus a little help from our friends — the birds and beneficial insects — keeps major invasions in check. If insects or disease appear to be beyond nature's control, however, follow the instructions in Chapter 8.

For appearance's sake, cut out the dead scapes after the flowers are gone, unless you are ripening some seeds you have hybridized or you plan to use the proliferations to start new plants (see Chapter 9).

Summer, when the daylilies are blooming, is an ideal time to tour other daylily gardens, check out the new introductions at nurseries, and talk with other growers about cultural methods. Taking a tour sponsored by a regional group of the American Hemerocallis Society is one of the best ways to do this. We enjoy these stimulating junkets, and we usually return to our own gardens inspired with many new ideas.

Fall Care

Tidy gardeners remove all the dead foliage and scapes from their daylilies after the plants have become dormant. Others, like us, prefer to leave the debris in place until spring, when it is easier to pull or rake it away. As we said before, we feel that it acts as a mulch and holds snow in place, both of which help protect the plants over winter if you live in a cold climate.

Most dormant cultivars are hardy enough so that they need no winter protection, but if you are growing evergreens and semi-evergreens, fall is the time to protect them with a winter cover if you live where temperatures drop below zero or fluctuate widely during the winter. If your climate provides a reliable snow cover and the temperature stays consistently cold all season, you probably do not need to cover dormant and semi-evergreen daylilies, for nature's insulation will be enough for them; but if you have evergreens, they will need protection.

Thick layers of hay, straw, leaves, or evergreen boughs, or the commercial plant-insulation blankets sold in garden-supply catalogs, all make good winter protection. However, don't cover the plants until just before the first hard freeze, if you can determine that time. If you cover too early, plants imported from an area with a longer growing season are likely to continue to grow under the mulch, and their new sprouts will be vulnerable to the extreme cold that will inevitably follow.

Solutions to Daylily Problems — A Checklist

Not Blossoming Well

❏ *Check shade and sun conditions.* You may need to move the plants or cut some branches off the trees that are shading the plants.

❏ *Too much fertilizer.* The plants may be getting burned; or perhaps they are growing too fast to bloom well. Very lush foliage but few blooms indicates that the plants may be too well fed.

❏ *Plants set too deep, or have sunk into the soil.* Raise the plants and reset.

❏ *Too much lime has locked up soil nutrients.* Avoid applying more lime or wood ashes for a few years.

❏ *Heavy seed production* the previous year may have weakened the plants.

❏ *Plants are overgrown and need to be divided.*

❏ *Plants are too small.* Give them a bit more fertilizer and another year.

❏ *Roots are too dry.* Increase the mulch and watering.

Not Growing Well

❏ *Plants are set too deep or not deep enough.* Reset.

❏ *Plants are overcrowded.* Divide, or move them to a spot where there is more room.

❏ *Weed or grass competition.* Remove it.

❏ *Mulch is too thick or too close to the plants.* Make necessary adjustments.

❏ *Need additional nutrients.* Apply manure dissolved in water or other liquid fertilizer. May also lack magnesium; add Epsom salts dissolved in water.

Erratic Growth, Cracked Stems, Discolored Foliage

❏ *Too much nitrogen.*

❏ *Overwatered.* Cut back on watering.

Insect or Disease Damage

See Chapter 8.

C H A P T E R   8

Daylily Pests and Their Control

AFTER FIGHTING PESTS in our vegetable garden and fruit orchard every year for as long as we can remember, we consider the daylily a gardener's dream plant. Most of the wild species are unusually resistant to both insects and diseases, and none are the favorite food of woodchucks, raccoons, rabbits, or deer. Although most new hybrids do not share all the pest immunity of their ancestors, they are free from the usual plant troubles. In fact, you may be able to grow these remarkable plants all your life and never need this chapter at all.

An established rule of nature is that the more plants of the same kind you grow together in one place, the more likely the chance that bugs and disease will set up residence there. Foresters warn about planting large acreages of all the same kind of trees, and gardeners find that as soon as they enlarge their plantings of any crop, their troubles also expand. Large plantings of daylilies are not excluded from this natural phenomenon and are likely to experience more difficulties than would a few lone plants scattered around the yard.

The severity of pest infestations often depends upon weather conditions. Diseases are more prevalent in a cool, damp summer, but insects proliferate faster in warm, dry years. It is difficult to know just what kind of a season to wish for, and some years, when we have first one extreme and then the other, we are doubly blessed with troubles! It is agreed that, in general, insects create the most trouble in warm areas where there is not a cold, hard winter to kill them off, and diseases are more prevalent in places with high humidity and in the North, where weather conditions fluctuate a great deal.

In the first few decades that we grew daylilies, no bugs seemed at all interested in our plantings. Then, in the late 1970s, the earwig discovered northern Vermont. Now, before we bring a bouquet into the house we shake it vigorously, and before we photograph a daylily we look it over carefully. More than once, just as we snapped a picture, an earwig crawled out of the throat, apparently wanting to be part of the show.

Although earwigs are all too easy to spot and identify, other daylily afflictions may not be as obvious. Every caring gardener, like a good parent observing his or her children, frequently looks over each plant and notices if something is not right — if the foliage is drooping or yellowing, whether it has spotty leaves, or perhaps buds that drop off before they open. When a symptom appears, it is important to correctly diagnose the problem before trying to remedy it.

It is tempting to blame a disease or insect for a plant's sorry appearance when the health problem may, instead, be caused by an environmental situation or physiological condition. Too much or too little moisture, fertilizer, or lime are potential suspects; or perhaps the misuse of a pesticide or weedkiller. An extreme of weather, such as drought, wind, or hail, can also ruin the appearance of completely healthy plants. Alternate thawing and freezing during the winter sometimes heaves young plants out of the ground and exposes their roots, drying them out. Sometimes the shade that results when young trees gradually grow and surreptitiously shut off the light can affect plants adversely. Plantings near a road may suffer damage when salt-treated ice melts in the springtime and runs onto the beds. Pollution from car and truck exhausts near a busy highway in summer may occasionally bother plants, too. Even an unnoticed sewer leak can affect the health of a planting.

It can be very frustrating when none of the obvious diseases, insects, or environmental problems seems to be the cause of a daylily's distress. When a new, expensive cultivar has a health problem, no one wants to dig it out and discard it. A friend of ours who has a large garden has a solution and keeps what he calls his "emergency ward" apart from the other plants. He moves any ailing daylilies or other perennials to this spot, where they are out of sight, but where he can observe them and give them special attention and exceptionally good soil. He reports that the recovery rate is very good. After a few weeks many of the patients are able to return to normal life in the border.

When environmental causes have been ruled out in the case of a sick-looking daylily, it is probably a disease or insect that is affecting its health. If more than a plant or two have problems, some kind of control is advisable.

Pest Control

Since daylilies, unlike wheat, corn, or fruit, are not a leading commercial crop in North America, comparatively little scientific research has been done relating to the causes and cures of the ailments that affect them. Much of the research to date has been done by members of the American Hemerocallis Society.

The insects that bother daylilies are the same as those that affect other perennials, so they can be controlled in the same ways recommended in general garden practice. The opinions of daylily growers about how best to control both insects and diseases seem to be evenly divided as to whether or not to use chemicals. Organic advocates believe in maintaining healthy plants by keeping the soil well supplied with organic nutrients and by encouraging the birds and beneficial insects that hold pests in check. Other growers feel it is nearly impossible to raise good daylilies without using at least a few chemicals to suppress insects and disease.

In most garden literature printed before 1940, arsenic, nicotine, and Paris green (a copper-arsenic compound) were recommended treatments for every nuisance, even for use on food plants. After World War II, the solution to every pest problem was DDT and a variety of similar products. Gardeners were told that the best way to prevent any possible pest from seeing the light of day was to start spraying early in the season and keep it up all summer. A garden shed well stocked with a variety of chemicals, dusters, and sprayers was the sign of an up-to-date gardener.

Then Rachel Carson's book *Silent Spring* made us all aware that preventative sprays were also killing off the ladybugs and birds that had formerly controlled many destructive bugs; in addition, she warned that pesticides cause cancer and other diseases, and pollute groundwater and streams. Finally, everyone began to take another look at pest control. With the old chemicals under suspicion, safer methods had to be found, and gardeners began to look for ways to prevent troubles before they started. The fledgling group of organic gardeners that

had been snickered at as smelly compost makers during the 1940s and 1950s suddenly were the vanguard.

"Integrated Pest Management," or IPM, as it is called, is currently in wide use as a method of controlling insects, disease, weeds, and other pests by a prevention-cure system. It is not always entirely "natural," though it may be accomplished completely by natural means. Organic gardeners try to attract birds, encourage the insects that consume aphids and other plant pests, and spray only with nontoxic soaps, diatomaceous earth, thuricide, and other similar products. Another group of gardeners also favor natural control methods, but they are not against using a chemical pesticide if a crisis demands it. They believe that the products presently on the market have been thoroughly tested before they were introduced and are safe if used as directed. Many use systemic pesticides because they believe that they have a less adverse effect on the surrounding air and soil than other chemical sprays, and one application is effective for the entire growing season.

Ask your Cooperative Extension Service or, in Canada, Agriculture Canada, or a local garden center or farm store about what is currently advised for your problem. A few pesticides have been known to damage daylilies, but compared to many other plants, they are quite tolerant of chemicals. Unfortunately, this tolerance has encouraged gardeners to use both insecticides and herbicides on them more freely and sometimes more carelessly than they would on other plants.

We recommend that you always try to control pests with natural methods first. In a small daylily garden you are likely never to have a serious problem with diseases or insects if you let nature take its course.

Still, although a few thrips or minor disfigurations from disease may not bother you or your plants in your own yard or private border, if you have a public display garden or sell plants, you will probably want to take some action. In the following descriptions of diseases and insects, we list controls for "worst-case scenarios."

Daylily Diseases

Because the summer browning of daylily foliage that is described in Chapter 7 appears to be a "condition" rather than a disease, it is not included in this list.

Bacterial Soft Rot

This disease is also often called crown rot. It is caused not by a virus or fungus, but by a bacteria that is present in many soils. A daylily's foliage, crown, and roots can all become infected rapidly, and the plant turns into a putrid, bad-smelling, mushy mess. The infection can enter the plant through a wound or natural opening, and if the moisture level is high, the disease may develop so quickly that the plant will die within a few days. Unfortunately, a plant may be already infected with this disease when it is sold, and it can spread through the soil to adjoining plants. Most nurseries are careful never to ship out sick plants, but

just in case, examine all shipments of new plants carefully, and quarantine in an isolated bed any that you suspect might be harboring a problem.

Soft rot is more troublesome in the South than in the North, but it can occur wherever temperatures and humidity levels are high, or if the soil is a trifle swampy. In overly moist conditions, consider planting your daylilies in raised beds, or mix enough sand with the soil so that it is adequately drained.

Once started, the disease is difficult to control, but when a valuable plant is infected, it is worthwhile to quickly apply an antibiotic such as streptomycin, which may help. Some growers sprinkle all their new plants with Comet cleanser or soak them in a solution of one part chlorine bleach to three parts water at planting time. Both do a good job of killing the bacteria.

At the first sign of soft rot in a growing plant, dig up the plant, remove any infected parts, treat the portion that is left with a chlorine bleach solution, and replant it in a new location. Sterilize the soil where you dug out the plant before setting out any new daylilies there. Ask your local extension service or Agriculture Canada for more information on soil sterilization.

Leaf Streak

When tan or brown streaks and spots appear on the leaves, and sometimes the entire leaf is discolored, leaf streak may have struck. This disease, widespread throughout the country, is caused by a fungus. Although it makes the plant look sick, it is not likely to kill it; but the loss of chlorophyll in the leaves may weaken it considerably. Some daylily cultivars are more susceptible to leaf streak than others, and the disease may disappear for a year or so and then return. About all you can do to remedy it is to remove the infected leaves for appearance's sake.

Mustard Seed Fungus

Mustard seed fungus is the culprit when masses of white material in cottonlike sheets or threadlike forms appear near the crown, followed by small, black or brown spores the size of mustard seeds on the leaves. Sometimes a plant turns completely yellow. This disease is sometimes called "southern blight," or "crown rot," though it is different from the bacterial soft rot just described. Quick treatment with a fungicide is recommended. Some gardeners advise digging up the entire plant and cutting off the top half of its foliage. They then soak the remaining clump in fungicide and replant it in a different location in case any spores are left in the soil. Before planting any new daylilies in that spot, it is prudent to sterilize the soil.

Spring Sickness

When a plant looks healthy in early spring but suddenly turns yellowish and stops growing, a mysterious disease called "spring sickness" should be suspected. It is most common in regions where spring arrives early but cold weather returns after the plants have begun to grow. Not much is known about the cause of this disease,

but certain cultivars and their offspring are extremely susceptible to it. Spring sickness usually affects only the inner leaves in a clump, but it can be bad enough to prevent the plant from making normal growth. Some scientists feel that spring sickness is caused by a fungus, and research is being done at the University of Vermont to identify it and search for a cure. At the present time, the only treatment that appears to help is to dig up the entire plant, carefully remove the infected inner leaves, and then replant it.

Yellows

A fungus disease that is currently showing up in parts of the Midwest can be identified by a strip of yellow in the foliage, and a gradual dieback of the top of the plant. Usually the plant recovers but is so weakened that it doesn't bloom until the following year. The usual remedy is to dig up the plant as soon as the first symptoms are noticed, treat it with a fungicide, and replant it.

Insects

Aphids

The aphid is one of several common insects that suck the juices from a plant and weaken it. The first sign of damage is often the changing of foliage color from green to yellow. Buds and blooms may also become deformed. White flecks, which are the shed skins of aphids, may also be noticeable on the leaves, and you may notice honeydew — a clear sticky sweet secretion of the aphids. Because honeydew attracts ants, they are usually in evidence as well. Daylily aphids are very tiny and bright green, and they are usually visible if you look carefully. When conditions are right, their fast reproduction assures that large numbers will spread through a garden in a short time.

Ants raise aphids for the sweet "honey" they secrete, and they pasture them out, like cattle, on plants. It is best not to spray infected daylily plants unless absolutely necessary, because aphids have natural insect enemies such as ladybugs. One of the best ways to control aphids is to destroy any ant colonies that may be building hills in the lawn nearby by drenching the hills with an insecticide. If it becomes absolutely necessary to spray the plants themselves to check serious infestations, use a soap solution (not a detergent) or a contact insecticide. Several treatments may be necessary as new eggs hatch, or as ant colonies introduce new aphids to their farm — your daylilies.

Beetles

Various kinds of beetles sometimes attack daylilies. Cucumber beetles chew holes in the buds, giving the flowers, when they bloom, a messy appearance. Japanese beetles feed on the flowers themselves, as well as the leaves and buds. The common method of control in a small planting is to pick off these large creatures by hand and drop them in a dish of kerosene, but spot spraying with a garden insecticide may be necessary if the infestation becomes large.

Cutworms

Climbing cutworms do their dirty work by riddling daylily leaves and buds. Because they feed only at night and hide in the soil and mulch during the day, they are difficult to spot. They are most active in springtime but may show up at other times of year as well. The moth is a lustrous brown shade, and the larvae are light brown with darker markings and a yellow dot on each segment. An insecticide soil drench is the best control.

Earwigs

Unless they are present in large numbers and chew holes in buds and flowers, earwigs usually do little damage to daylilies; but, like a skunk in the backyard, their very presence is a nuisance. They annoy us especially when they hitch a ride into the house and create a panic. They are difficult to control because the insecticides that we consider safe have little effect on them, and they appear to have no natural enemies. Even the birds don't seem to eat them.

These insects did not arrive on this continent until the early 1900s, when they first appeared in Rhode Island. Since then they have invaded most of the continent, traveling on plants, vegetables, and vehicles until they have become well known and despised almost everywhere. Hybridizers, especially, find them a problem when they damage the blooms of prized cultivars right after they have been pollinated.

Picking them from the flowers with tweezers is practical in a small garden, but not in large plantings. Some gardeners lay down two wide, slightly moistened boards on top of each other, kept slightly apart by small sticks. When the insects crawl between the boards to escape the summer sun, they can be easily crushed by quickly removing the sticks and pressing the boards together.

Leafhoppers

Like aphids, these miniature broad jumpers suck juices from the plant without causing any noticeable injury until the foliage begins to appear discolored and weakened. Unlike aphids, they move rapidly from plant to plant, especially when disturbed. Because of their prolific breeding habits and speedy movements, they can quickly infest an entire planting. To control them, a mild insecticide such as pyrethrum (a product made from a daisylike perennial of the same name) is worth a try, as is a solution of soapy (not detergent) water. Chemical controls may be necessary if the situation becomes epidemic.

Millipedes

These insects are seldom a problem, since they ordinarily eat only dead and decaying vegetation. They attack live plants only when their numbers build up to much larger than normal proportions. In this unlikely event, as a last resort, drench the soil around the plant with insecticide.

Nematodes

Since nematodes work on the plant roots and are minute in size, the only inkling you would have that these tiny soil insects are working underground is the deteriorating condition of your plants. Like aphids, there are numerous species, and daylilies are not usually their targets, although they attack many other kinds of plants. Nematodes are present in every part of the country but are far more common in areas with long growing seasons and mild winters, where deep frosts do not kill them. They are difficult to control once they have become established in an area, and if they have taken up residence, it may be necessary to sterilize the soil before planting. Some gardeners have had good luck in repelling them, at least partially, by drenching the soil with a solution of Epsom salts, or by growing African-type marigolds with smelly blooms and foliage among the daylilies.

Slugs

Although they are not true insects, slugs sometimes feed on  dormant plants during a mild winter, and in early spring they chew holes in the new leaves as soon as they sprout. Like many insects, they feed at night and stay out of sight during the daytime. Cool, damp organic mulches are their favorite hiding places because they need such conditions to survive. Since sunlight and dry, rough surfaces are uncomfortable for slugs, some gardeners spread sand or coarse gravel around their plants as a repellent. Because of their terrific reproductive ability, the highly touted "saucer of beer in the garden" method of controlling them is of doubtful use, although it does attract and drown small numbers efficiently. Collecting slugs under moist boards and squashing them is a messy solution, but it works. Some country gardeners raise a few ducks for slug control since they have a reputation for finding the slimy creatures tasty! Chemical sprays or powders formulated especially for slug control may be necessary in extreme infestations.

Spider Mites

Mites suck the chlorophyll from daylily foliage, causing it to lose its rich green color. The leaves turn a dull brown and eventually die, greatly weakening the plant. These tiny, barely visible insects sometimes cover the plants with a fine webbing which helps to identify their presence, but a magnifying glass is necessary to be positive. Mites can be particularly devastating to daylilies during hot, dry summers, and some growers have found that running mist sprinklers over their daylily beds at night helps to slow down a rapid population buildup. When there is a major invasion of the creatures, it may become necessary to use a miticide.

Tarnished Plant Bug

The tarnished plant bug works on the tips of the flower buds, and their activities prevent the flower from opening properly. The creatures are only ¼ inch long and have a winged body of several mottled colors. They usually feed first on the leaf buds of nearby trees and then go on to chew a wide variety of vegetable and flower plants. Control is difficult because they breed frequently (five generations during a summer is not unusual). When natural controls appear not to be keeping them in check, frequent spraying or dusting may be the only way to cope.

Thrips

Thrips are one of the most common daylily problems. The small insects bore into the buds to extract the liquid there, and as the buds bleed, the liquid makes the petals adhere to each other so the flowers cannot open properly. Those that open all the way are likely to have white blemishes on their petals.

Even though thrips are tiny, they are large enough to see under close examination. During the years when they are around in large numbers, the amount of damage they cause can be reason for alarm.

Spray with almost any insecticide to control thrips. If they are an annual problem, it is worthwhile to begin to spray the plants as soon as growth starts in the spring.

Wasps

Although wasps do not usually damage daylilies, occasionally they feed on buds in the summer and damage seedpods in the fall. Control is seldom necessary, however.

Other Pests

Different years bring different challenges to daylily growers. Sometimes grasshoppers, spittlebugs, or other creatures arrive in larger than usual numbers, or bigger pests can cause worrisome damage. Birds sometimes break off the scapes of our finest blooms by alighting on them, even though the branches of surrounding trees would be a less precarious perch. (Some growers provide bird roosts throughout the garden to help eliminate breakage, but we are not sure how successful a ploy it is.) We are certainly in favor of encouraging the birds to stay in the neighborhood, even though we may lose a few buds.

Since daylilies are edible, it is surprising that so few animals bother them, although deer sometimes do. In fact, Lee Bailey says in his book *Country Flowers* that he plants daylilies as a barrier to keep rabbits away from the tasty members of the *Lilium* genus which they love. The rabbits do not cross through the daylily foliage to get to them.

Moles are probably the biggest nuisance. Their tunnels loosen the soil, causing daylily roots to dry out; and mice may use the openings as throughways to get to the roots, which they like to nibble on. As we said before, spreading mothballs in their burrows often makes the creatures move away. Some gardeners have reported successful mole control by placing Juicy Fruit gum in their holes, claiming that it gums up the animal's digestive system and proves fatal to them; but not everyone is convinced that this method works. Although moles do not make tasty eating for cats, we once had a good huntress who caught them for sport and brought them to us in return for our praise. Unfortunately, she usually chose to do this when we had company, probably so more people could admire them.

Beneficial Insects

In the checks and balances of nature, several insects are friends to gardeners, and their presence is an important reason for not spraying toxic materials and for trying to get your neighbors to avoid spraying, too. Among the good guys are the following:

Ground Beetles

Most people fail to recognize these large insects as friends. Their bodies, ridged lengthwise, are an iridescent brown or dull black in color, and they run rapidly but do not fly. Both the beetles and their larvae eat caterpillars of all types.

Lacewing Flies

These pale green flies have lacy, netted wings. They lay their eggs on other insects, and the larvae then consume the insects.

Ladybugs

Ladybugs are such well-known aphid eaters that they are often advertised in magazines for that purpose. However, as the old poem suggests, they "fly away," and so a new batch of imported ladybugs may not linger in your garden long enough to be useful on a long-term basis unless your beds are overwhelmed with aphids. The ladybugs, however, usually stay around long enough to be helpful and to add a bit of cheerful color to the garden. The best way to encourage those you already have is to avoid spraying.

Praying Mantis

The impressive size and unusual appearance of these creatures makes them interesting, but to some, unfortunately, they seem a frightening addition to the garden. They are also well-known consumers of aphids as well as other unfriendly insects; and their huge brown egg cases, which appear in the fall, are a welcome sight in the vicinity of any planting. They do not usually survive the winter in cold areas, but fortunately they thrive in regions where they are most needed. Like ladybugs, they can be found listed for sale in the classified columns of garden magazines.

Syrphid Flies

Also known as the hover fly, this tiny fly frequents flowers for their nectar and sometimes pollinates them as well. They are best identified by their habit of hovering over flowers with rapidly vibrating wings. Their larvae feed on aphids, and unless you find that they interfere with your hybridizing, it is best not to get rid of them.

Tachinid Flies

Horseflies, as these insects are often called, have iridescent wings and are gray-black in color. They attach their eggs to other insects, where the larvae hatch and subsequently consume their hosts. One strain of this fly was introduced into North America to help in the control of the gypsy moth.

CHAPTER 9

Starting New Plants from Your Daylilies

"Mistress Mary always felt that however many years she lived she should never forget that first morning when her garden began to grow."

—Frances Hodgson Burnett, *The Secret Garden*

PLANTING A SEED the size of a pepper-corn and seeing it transformed into a glorious daylily plant can be an exhilarating experience. We find it quite exciting to act as midwives in this miracle of nature, and when a new plant gives birth to its first lovely blossom, you'd think we had created it ourselves!

Like most plants, daylilies can be propagated in several different ways. The two most common are by planting seeds and by dividing the plants. Lesser used methods of propagating plants include the use of proliferations — the little plants or slips that occasionally form on the daylily scapes about the time it blooms — and tissue culture, the modern, laboratory method of cloning. Offsets and root cuttings are seldom used to propagate daylilies except in the case of certain stoloniferous species, such as the Tawny Daylily, *Hemerocallis fulva*, and their closely related cultivars 'Europa', 'Kwanso', and 'Flore Pleno', all of which rapidly form new plants at the ends of their roots. These rooted offshoots can be severed and transplanted.

Division ensures that the new plants will be carbon copies of the parent, identical cultivars, whereas plants grown from seed are never the same as their parents. If a clump of 'Manila Moon' is divided into five plants, for example, each will still be a 'Manila Moon'; but if all the seeds from a pod of 'Manila Moon' are planted, they will develop into entirely different plants, and like humans, each will inherit a different combination of all the different characteristics of its many ancestors. Proliferations, offsets, and root cuttings all produce clones of the same plant.

Dividing Daylilies

Dividing daylily clumps is the easiest and most common way for a home gardener to start new plants. Not only are you sure that each division will be like the parent, but the new little plants will get off to a good start because they are already acclimated to your garden.

For many reasons, we like to divide daylilies when they are coming to life in the spring. The sprouts are obvious then, so we can be sure of getting a few fans and enough roots on each division. The leaves are short at that time, and don't require a lot of water to nourish them. The lack of tall masses of leaves and flower stems also makes it easy to see what you are doing. The soil is usually damp in the spring, which is another thing in the plant's favor. Spring-divided plants re-establish themselves quickly, and if you do not make the divisions too small, they are likely to bloom the first year.

Spring isn't the only time that plants can be divided successfully, however. When necessary, even on a warm summer day, we split up large plants of the older cultivars when they are in bloom and transplant the divisions. We prefer not to do this with the best cultivars because there is a certain amount of risk involved with less vigorous plants. However, many gardeners feel there is no problem with divid-

ing any plant whenever you want, if you use normal precautions. Southern growers can divide their plants safely almost anytime when the weather isn't too dry.

A large, healthy clump of daylilies can be split into several pieces using a sharp thrust of a round-pointed spade driven straight down into the clump while it is still in the ground. If you want your new plants to develop quickly into blooming-size clumps, each daylily division you make should include at least three or four fans.

When you want to leave part of the clump intact to keep growing in place, chip away pieces of it from the outside edge. The undisturbed portion should continue to bloom well, even the first summer after division. Do not cut away at a clump haphazardly, but do it carefully, or you're likely to come up with a shovelful of foliage but no crown or roots.

When it is more important to get as many new plants as possible than to get blooming-size divisions, dig up the clump completely and wash off the soil so you can see all the individual plant segments or fans before separating them. Then carefully cut the fans apart with a knife. Since divisions with only one or two fans are fragile and somewhat weak, dust the cut ends with a fungicide before planting them so they will not become infected.

Most gardeners, when faced with a large clump, first split it in half as if they were cutting a pie. Then they split each half in two pieces, and continue to divide it in this manner as long as they can still make divisions that are large enough to produce blooming-size plants. It is easier to get a good amount of leaves and roots on each division by doing it this way rather than by chipping pieces off a large clump.

Some cultivars can be easily separated by pulling apart the different segments by hand, but the crowns of others are so brittle that it is necessary to work with great care if you attempt it. Growers who divide daylilies without a knife feel they have better luck getting the necessary sprouts and roots on each division if they pry the fans apart with a screwdriver or narrow chisel.

It is tempting, when you have a superior daylily, to try to start a lot of new plants from a small clump. We watched in amazement one hot July day in full sun as a skilled professional nurseryman with a sharp knife separated a medium-size clump into thirty divisions, each with roots and sprouts. Since he intended to grow them for a year before he sold them, the large yield was fine for his business. Most of us, however, are more interested in getting blooming-size clumps quickly than in nursing along a lot of small, weak plants.

After you have split up a clump, plant the new divisions as you would any new mail-order plant, as described in Chapter 6.

Speeding Up Production

Propagators are always searching for ways to speed up production of daylily clumps, using techniques that range from high-tech

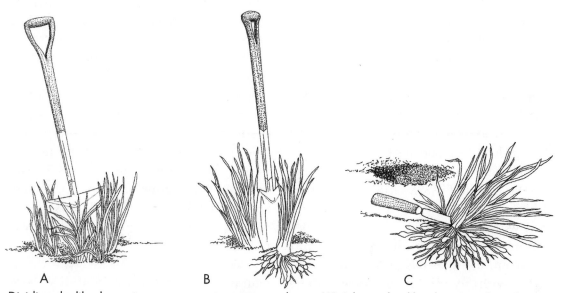

A   B   C

Dividing daylily clumps is an easy way to start new plants. (A) A large, healthy clump can be split into several pieces with a sharp thrust of a spade driven straight down into the clump while it is still in the ground; (B) a single fan or two can be chipped away from the outside edge without disturbing the rest of the clump; or (C) the entire clump may be dug up and the fans cut apart with a knife.

to New Age. Using additional fertilizer is a common way, as you might guess, since in plant production, increasing the number of fans quickly is more important than producing flowers. Some propagators set the plants in the ground at a level slightly less deep than they would other daylilies, so that the crowns are barely above the soil line. They believe that this level of planting encourages the plant to spread more easily and produce more fans. Other gardeners cut back the foliage to about 2 inches above the ground after the plant has bloomed, claiming that it results in an increased number of fans as the plant tries to replace its lost foliage. The use of chemicals appeals to some, and they dissolve birth control pills or DMSO with water and apply it to the soil around the plants to make the fans propagate more rapidly. DMSO is a product used by veterinarians on animals for lameness and other ailments. Since it is not approved for use on humans, it is not easy to obtain, but it can be bought for plant use. Some of our New Age friends call on nature's *devas* for assistance, consult astrology charts before planting, or grow their plants under pyramids or near quartz crystals to get optimum proliferation.

In *Wyman's Gardening Encyclopedia*, Donald Wyman describes two processes that can be used to increase the number of fans a daylily produces each year. One method is to cut off the top of the plant in the spring when it is dormant and scoop out the crown, leaving a rim of crown tissue; new buds subsequently form on the roots around the rim. After these tiny plants have developed good root systems, they are divided, moved to a transplant bed, and grown there until they have become large enough to plant in the garden.

Another way to increase daylilies is to split a daylily leaf down into, but not through, the crown of the plant and to separate the pieces with slivers of wood or plastic. This often causes a single fan to divide into two or more.

Although some gardeners have reported good results using both of these methods, we have never found any great difference in the speed with which mutilated plants propagate, compared with that of well-fertilized plants that were not damaged. We continue to propagate our plants by simple division without using any methods to speed up their growth except to keep them growing well by maintaining their soil in good condition and giving them plenty of water. We find that many variables affect the speed of growth, including the vigor of the cultivar and the weather conditions, both of which are beyond our control. Sometimes we can separate a three-year-old clump into twenty-five new segments, and sometimes into only two, but the average is five to ten.

Propagating by Proliferations

Proliferations are small plants, or slips, that occasionally develop about midway up the scape of a daylily about blooming time; they actually look like miniature daylily plants.

Some cultivars develop them readily, and sometimes you'll find several growing on one plant, but other cultivars never produce them. Rooting proliferations and nurturing them into maturity is an interesting way to increase a supply of scarce cultivars that do not form clumps rapidly.

This method of propagation works best where growing seasons are long, because proliferations tend to form late in the season and it takes time for them to develop a good root system, which they must do before cold weather appears. Northern gardeners have to be content to propagate only the daylilies that bloom early and in midseason in this manner or in some way

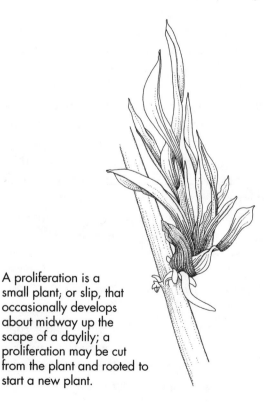

A proliferation is a small plant, or slip, that occasionally develops about midway up the scape of a daylily; a proliferation may be cut from the plant and rooted to start a new plant.

protect their plants from frost. Some gardeners grow stock plants in large pots so they can move them to a greenhouse when frost threatens.

After a proliferation is well developed, carefully sever it from the plant with an extremely sharp knife or a razor blade and then root it as you would any cutting. Gardeners differ about the best way to cut off a proliferation. Most of us just shave it off, taking a small chunk of stem with it. Others wait until the plant stops blooming and then cut off the entire scape; they then cut off the parts of the scape just above and below the section with the proliferation on it and plant the proliferation with the small portion of the scape attached. They claim that roots form faster on such a cutting.

A variety of media can be used successfully for the rooting process, but, like all cuttings, proliferations form roots best in one that is light, such as sandy soil or various combinations of perlite, vermiculite, and peat moss. We prefer a sterile mixture of half perlite and half vermiculite. The rooting can be done in either flats or small pots, but pots are easier to label and keep track of when you are propagating only a few proliferations of several different varieties.

To speed up the rooting process, many growers dust the cut end of the proliferation with a chemical such as Rootone after removing it from the scape; others prefer to dust the base of the proliferation where it is still attached to the plant before removing it. They feel that early treatment with a rooting powder (a week or two before re-

STARTING NEW PLANTS **101**

moval) stimulates faster development of the roots after the proliferation has been cut off and planted. In addition to rooting compounds, other chemicals such as Lanolin BAP-IAA are sometimes used to encourage root development. (For sources, see the Appendix.)

Soak the rooting medium thoroughly, before inserting the proliferations, and never let it dry out completely during the time the plant is rooting. Some propagators recommend soaking the proliferations in slightly warm water for a few hours so they will be turgid when they are stuck into the sand or other rooting medium. Stick the cut ends of the proliferations at least ¾ inch deep into the medium and then label them. Cover the tops of the pots or flats with a sheet of lightweight plastic film, and keep the plants warm (between 70° and 80°F.) and in light but out of direct sunlight until they form roots. The first roots should form within a few weeks, and the plants should be nicely developed and well rooted within two months; then transplant them into a light potting soil.

In areas with long growing seasons, proliferations can be rooted outdoors, but in the short summers of the North it works best to do it in a warm house or greenhouse. Once the plants are rooted heavily, they can spend the winter in a greenhouse, or a cold frame if they are mulched. As soon as the weather warms in the spring, all the healthy little plants can be transplanted to outdoor beds, but the weaker ones should grow on in their pots or in the cold frame for a few additional weeks.

Tissue Culture

When tissue culture was first introduced, the cloning of plants in the laboratory created a great deal of excitement, and many predicted that eventually all plants would be started commercially by this method. In theory, in-vitro production assures that plants will be reproduced quickly, by the millions if needed, and that each plant will be healthy and vigorous because it is completely disease free.

Tissue culture is a fascinating process: A tiny piece of plant, often part of a growing bud, is sterilized and placed in a test tube in a sterile chemical mixture that has been carefully formulated for each plant species, and sometimes for each cultivar. Temperature, humidity, and pH are all carefully controlled, and the water and air entering the area are sterilized. Under these conditions the plant tissue grows rapidly. When enough of it has been produced, it is removed from the tube and carefully cut into small pieces, each of which is placed in a larger test tube or beaker containing a different solution. Here the tissue mass grows tops and roots and becomes a small plant. At this stage, it can be transplanted either into the ground or into a flat or pot for further development before it is sold. In winter, plants are grown in a greenhouse, making year-round production possible.

Tissue culture has obvious advantages over conventional kinds of propagation. Plants can be rapidly propagated throughout the year. It eliminates the need for huge numbers of stock plants, since the tissue can be stored for long periods in its first stage, until needed. When orders demand it, the technician removes the tissue from storage and produces the desired number of vigorous, healthy, virus-free plants.

This high-tech process is already being widely used to propagate a variety of plants that are in great demand, such as strawberries, raspberries, blueberries, and other small fruits. Others being produced in huge numbers include hedge plants, orchids, dwarfing stock for fruit trees, and houseplants.

Tissue culture of certain perennials, including daylilies, has not been as successful, because mutations have taken place frequently enough in test tubes or propagation jars during the cloning process so that many growers have become wary of the process. No one is absolutely sure why a golden-yellow 'Hudson Valley' can change into a plant that produces small, washed-out maroon flowers, but it appears that some cultivars are more unstable than others. Some believe that mutation occurs when sanitary conditions are not closely monitored; others believe it happens more frequently when plants that were themselves created by tissue culture are used for culturing new plants. Some nurseries appear to have solved the problems and are propagating true-to-name plants consistently, but many gardeners, having encountered bad results in the past, are cautious about buying tissue-cultured plants.

The technology is so new that opinions vary about whether tissue-cultured daylilies are more healthy and vigorous than other plants. Since the plants are initially healthy and virus free, the young plants seem to be more resistant than conventionally propagated plants to spring sickness and other diseases; but skeptics believe that, like humans, they may later on be even more susceptible to pests because they have never built up a natural resistance to them. Some also feel that any cultured plant material held in storage in the laboratory for long periods loses its hardiness. The jury is still out on these questions.

Tissue-cultured plants are comparable in price to field-propagated specimens, but when purchased by mail they are usually smaller, although they tend to grow rapidly after they are planted. When tissue culture becomes a more common method for propagating named cultivars, we will undoubtedly see the end of the era in which a new cultivar can remain for years in the $50 price category. Another possible result of this bonanza, however, is that a few large growers may dominate the nursery business and offer only a limited number of cultivars.

Growing Daylilies from Seed

If you don't mind having unnamed daylilies in your garden, you can grow your own beautiful specimens from hybrid seed purchased from a seed catalog or collected from your own or a neighbor's patch. Some seed companies sell tetraploid seeds, and these might be the most interesting to try, but diploids, too, are perfectly satisfactory. If you want to save seed from your own cultivars, look for pods that have formed as a result of accidental pollination, or do your own cross-pollination. (See Chapter 10 for details about hybridizing your own seed, and the Appendix for commercial seed sources.) The process takes patience because you must wait at least two years for the first blooms, and probably another year or two before the plants form a good clump and produce well-developed flowers. If all goes well, however, you will end up with dozens of good daylilies for less than the price you might pay for a single plant, and you'll have fun in the bargain.

If you want vigorous plants that are especially suitable for covering banks and other difficult places, select seeds from the species or early cultivars. They usually set seed in large amounts, and you can pick and dry them after they have turned brown. Often they scatter their own seed, which you might think would indicate that the seeds could simply be scattered over the area where you want plants to grow, but from experience we have found that this method is seldom successful. Planting seeds in flats or beds is a much more certain way of obtaining new plants.

If you live in the North, you may have an additional reason for growing daylilies from seed. Northern gardeners have found that they can sometimes grow the tender evergreens that are so popular in milder climates if they plant seeds instead of buying plants. Apparently the seedlings are better able to adapt to the cool climates.

Don't expect every plant grown from seed, even seed from the very best cultivars, to produce prizewinning blooms. A large percentage of seedlings are usually well worth the trouble of growing them, however. When we get a hundred seedlings from the crossing of our best daylilies, we are delighted if twenty are really good ones, forty fairly good, and twenty worth putting on a wild roadside. That leaves about twenty to end up on the compost pile. We dare to hope that there will be one in a few hundred that is worth naming and registering.

If you wish to start daylilies from seed, pick mature pods that have turned brown and begun to split open. The one on the left is ready to harvest. Put the pods in a warm, dry place until they are dry.

Seed Treatment

Daylilies are not as easy to start as radishes or marigolds because their hard-shelled seeds do not readily soften and allow moisture to penetrate the interior. They also need a chilling period in order to break their dormancy and germinate well. Each grower has a favorite method of starting seeds, and you may want to experiment to find what works best for you. Nature does most of her planting in late summer and fall, and some growers plant their daylilies then, too. They sow the seeds as soon as they pick them, before the seed coating has become tough, and then allow the flats to chill outdoors for a few weeks before bringing them indoors to grow during the winter. Many southern gardeners plant the seeds directly in the ground, where the seeds remain dormant over the winter and sprout in the spring.

We like to dry the seeds we raise ourselves (see Chapter 10) and plant them in midwinter, when the lengthening days will stimulate fast growth. After the seeds have been stored for a time, we give them the same chilling treatment they would get if they had been planted outside in the fall. We seal them in a plastic bag and store them in the refrigerator (not the freezer) for four to eight weeks. We also give purchased seed the same cold treatment.

In late January, we take the seeds from the refrigerator and plant them immediately. To speed up germination, some people soak the chilled seed in slightly warm water for a few hours before planting, and others carefully peel or nick the hard coating of each seed with a knife.

Planting

There are many ways of starting seeds, and after trying numerous methods, we have found that the following one is successful for us: We plant the chilled seed in a standard-size nursery flat (about 10" x 20" x 2"), filling it to about ½ inch from the top with an artificial soil mix such as Grow-Mix or Pro-Mix. We prefer these mixes to garden soil because they are sterile and thus are free from weed seeds and disease organisms. Before planting we wet the mix thoroughly with slightly warmed water, which takes time because artificial soils absorb moisture slowly.

The seeds can be scattered over the top of the mix, but we prefer to mark off rows spaced about ¾ inch apart and plant methodically. We place the large seeds about ½ inch apart in the rows and then cover the entire surface with a ¼-inch layer of horticultural perlite. We could use artificial soil for this purpose, but perlite dries out faster, which helps keep the seedlings from getting damping-off diseases.

We water the seed trays frequently, but never too generously at any one time, and let the perlite dry between waterings. As we have said, artificial soil can absorb a great deal of moisture, and if the soil is soggy, the roots can't easily grow. We always warm the water just enough to take off the chill and use a bulb-type sprinkler so the force of the water won't wash out the seeds or damage the frail, young seedlings as they sprout. If you do not have a rubber-bulb sprinkler made especially for watering seedlings, a plastic bottle designed for sprinkling clothes works just as well.

It is important to keep the seed trays at a temperature of 70° to 75°F. day and night for the first few weeks. Around-the-clock use of fluorescent grow-lights makes it easy to control the temperature, because the bulbs give off just enough heat to keep the soil mix warm, and the long period of light helps the seeds germinate faster. Ordinary fluorescent bulbs are satisfactory as long as the seedlings also get sunlight from windows for part of the day; but if the flats are to remain under the lights for weeks with no natural light, it is better to use daylight-type bulbs that provide the full-spectrum light the plants need.

Daylilies can also be started in a sunny window, but because a warm temperature is so necessary, it is best to move them away from a cool window at night and put them near a radiator, stove, or other heat source that is warm but not hot.

Even with the best of care, daylily seeds sprout very unevenly, and there are always some that never germinate. Allow at least two weeks for the first sprouts to appear, and at least six weeks before you resign yourself to the fact that the ones you now have are all you're likely to get. Breeders frequently tell of tossing out flats of ungerminated seeds, only to find them happily growing in the compost pile weeks later.

Gardeners try all sorts of methods to improve germination and help their tiny seedlings. Some use a solution of water and DMSO (see page 99); other growers report improved germination and growth by dissolving birth control pills in water and sprinkling the seedlings. Still others claim good results from carrying on cheery daily conversations with their seedlings. Of course, there are also those gardeners who do not use any of the above methods but concentrate on watering the seedlings carefully and maintaining a constant warm temperature for them. We belong to this latter group, but we are careful never to say an unkind word to the plants, just in case.

Seedling Diseases

Daylily seedlings are not nearly as likely as other plants to succumb to the damping-off diseases that so often wipe out whole plantings of petunia and begonia seedlings just as they are beginning to grow well, but there is always a chance that it may happen.

The most common damping-off diseases that affect seedlings are caused by the fungi *Pithium, Fusarium, Rhizoctonia,* and *Phytophthora.* They are most likely to attack newly emerged plants that are stressed by dampness and cold, weakened by overcrowding, or suffering from too much or too little fertilizer. After the plants have grown 1 or 2 inches high, there is less danger of damping off, and the nightly temperature can be lowered to 60°F., but still allow the tops of the plants to dry thoroughly between waterings.

If, in spite of your care, you see damping-off symptoms such as the browning of the plant stems near the bottom, or if the plants suddenly wilt and fall over, immediately apply a fungicide to check the disease or you may lose the seedlings.

After-Care of Seedlings

Even after the young plants have grown for several months, they are usually still small. In late winter we transplant them so each will have enough space to develop a sturdy root system before it is set out in the garden.

Handle the seedlings carefully, because their roots are often straggly and extremely fragile. Transplant them into flats filled with good potting soil and space them about 2 inches apart, or if you have only a few, you may prefer to use small, individual pots. Water them whenever they look dry, and feed them once a week with a weak solution of liquid fertilizer. Don't plant them outdoors until all danger of frost is past, and before you put them in the ground, set the flats outside in a sheltered spot for a few sunny days to harden them up. Then transplant them into outdoor beds of thoroughly prepared, light soil. Space them 6 to 8 inches apart, firming the soil around each one so it won't sink into the ground, and mulch them with a light material such as cocoa shells or finely shredded bark. Keep the plants watered, and allow them to remain in the bed until they start to bloom.

When the seedlings blossom, you can weed out any that look hopelessly bad, so the promising ones will have more room to grow; or you can move all the best plants to another row or bed. Southern growers, with their long growing season, can usually evaluate their seedlings in a couple of years, but northerners need to allow an additional year or two to observe all of their good and bad points and to thoroughly check out their growing and flowering habits. By then it is clear which ones are worth a permanent place in the garden.

Our daylily seedling beds create a lot of interest, both for us and our nursery customers. Sometimes the customers want to buy seedlings instead of the many lovely named cultivars we have for sale. When the new plants begin to bloom for the first time, every day brings new surprises, and we can hardly wait to see what will burst forth next.

C H A P T E R 10

The Fun of Originating New Cultivars

WHEN WE LOOK AT PHOTOS of all the lovely new daylily introductions each year and realize that many of them were created by hybridizers in small backyards, it is easy to wonder, "Why not me, too?"

With more than 32,000 *Hemerocallis* already registered, one might think the world could not possibly need any more. Yet in spite of the beauties now available, each new cultivar, like a new baby, is unique; and the challenge to create new beauty does not stop simply because beauty already exists. Furthermore, the "perfect" daylily has not yet been developed.

Hybridizing is a fascinating gamble, and the best part of it is that you can't lose. Whether or not you ever hit the jackpot and develop a distinctly terrific daylily, you'll certainly come up with a number of beautiful "almosts," many of which you'll be proud to display in your garden. And if you *should* get a plant that is superior in some way to any other, you'll join the ex-

clusive ranks of the recognized daylily hybridizers. Then, too, there is always the pipe dream of possible financial reward. No one can guess what the first giant, ruffled, true-blue daylily will sell for, but we know it won't be in the $5 class for many years.

Most new cultivars of a couple of decades ago were the results of the haphazard crossing of two reasonably good daylilies, often by amateur hybridizers. The parents were usually chosen because the flowers looked nice in the garden and the plants set seed easily. After serious interest in daylily growing began and regular flower-judging contests started among clubs in the American Hemerocallis Society, breeders concentrated on developing plants with large, showy flowers that would win awards. Pinks, reds, and yellows were especially popular, and later on, the near-whites and those with blends of several colors.

The search for prizewinning blooms produced some stunning cultivars, but as hybridizers introduced flowers that were more showy, they often overlooked other desirable plant characteristics. Many times the plants were too tall for flower beds and home landscaping, or they lacked the vigor and disease-resistance of the earlier species and cultivars. Recently, however, as many hybridizers have realized that they may have gone about as far as they can with colors and color combinations, there has been more concentration on things that ordinary gardeners feel are more important. Often catalogs now detail bud count, blooming habits, and pest resistance as well as flower beauty.

Scientific Breeding

Some breeders still take an unscientific approach to plant development and depend mostly on luck. They simply cross some of their favorite cultivars with each other and occasionally come up with a good descendant, even though they seldom know who the parents are. Most successful modern hybridizers, however, know exactly what they are looking for and plan every step accordingly. They are extremely knowledgeable about the traits of the breeding stock they use and aim toward combining the characteristics of many plants to get their desired results. Some hybridizers may work to enhance flower fragrance, to create ruffles and fancy edgings, or to develop unusual color combinations such as bright, contrasting blotches. Others may want to include a shiny glow or a powdery, sparkling "diamond dust" overcast on the petals of their new developments. Although they keep very good records and work with care, most admit that, in spite of all their planning, success still depends to a great extent on luck. The number of possible combinations of daylily genes is astronomical.

As in the fashion world, fads and styles in daylilies change, and hybridizers try to keep pace. The demand has lessened for the giant pink blooms so popular a few years ago; now there is a great deal of interest in dwarf, small-flowering, miniature daylilies. Almost-whites and near-blues are big sellers among the connoisseurs, as are flowers with contrasting blotches and unusual edgings.

A new seedling that produces only seven or eight blooms to a scape, stunning though they may be, is no longer good enough for most originators. More desirable is a sturdy plant that produces, each day for several weeks, a number of nicely formed, sun-fast flowers high above a mass of healthy green foliage. Backyard gardeners would like to have more plants available that open their blossoms wide early in the morning, even after a cold night, and stay in bloom for a few hours after dark. Some breeders are seeking flowers that open in late afternoon and continue to bloom all the next day. Others are certain that someday there will be *Hemerocallis* plants producing blooms that stay open for several days without fading. No one has suggested what we will call this new breed of plants, however; certainly the name "daylily" would no longer fit.

Serious hybridizers always have a plan,

or a program, as it is called. For example, you might have as a goal a cultivar that is a dormant, miniature pink with a green-yellow throat, and perhaps you also want it to produce forty buds on each scape. The next step would be to collect cultivars that have the characteristics you want to accentuate in your new creation.

It is likely that numerous generations of daylilies will be needed to successfully combine the characteristics of many different plants in one daylily, unless a hybridizer is very lucky. The breeding process is faster for those who live in the southern states because the long growing season below the Mason-Dixon Line makes it possible for a plant to mature faster, so several additional generations can be crowded into a twenty-year period.

High-tech Hybridizing

High tech has become part of the plant breeding world, as it has the rest of our everyday lives. Not only has tissue culture resulted in test-tube propagation, but many other plant developments are taking place in laboratories, where hybridizers wear white, sterile suits instead of dirty overalls. They can now create startling mutations by transplanting genes from one cell to another through the use of chemicals and disease organisms. In an attempt to develop the elusive blue daylily, for example, scientists have moved genes from completely unrelated species, such as blue petunias, into the chromosomes of daylilies. Although it

may upset purists when the natural processes of plant breeding are bypassed, the wheels of progress are not likely to be stopped by their protests. Even the most conservative gardener will likely feel a sense of excitement when the first blue daylily appears, even if it is wearing blue genes.

Among the many laboratory advances in the past half-century is the discovery of how to convert diploid daylilies to tetraploids. As we said earlier, colchicine is a deadly alkaloid extracted from the autumn crocus, *Colchicine autumnale,* and is used to double the usual twenty-two chromosomes in each daylily cell to forty-four.

You don't need to work in a lab to create tetraploids (or "tets"). To bring about the conversion, the colchicine is mixed with water and applied either to sprouting seeds, small seedlings, or to the buds of mature plants when they are just beginning to grow in the spring. Application is repeated for three or four days, after which the chemical is carefully washed from the plant with water.

Accurate dosages are necessary, since too little colchicine results in no conversion and too much kills the seedlings or plants outright. Half-conversions, which are common, result in plants called chimeras. Unfortunately these are not always recognized, and consequently, chimeras have occasionally been propagated and sold as tetraploids.

There was a great deal of interest in the tetraploid conversion of many different kinds of flowers when the process first began to produce sensational results with bearded iris. Soon after, nearly every daylily hybridizer was ready to get in on the action, too. Although many small-time breeders are still creating tets, presently fewer than a dozen of the leading daylily hybridizers are making conversions an active part of their program. Most others now prefer to take advantage of the more than 5,000 tetraploids already developed — doubles, miniatures, spiders, and giant blooming types — which are available. Colchicine, once readily available to experimenters both in liquid and tablet form, is now more difficult to buy, although some companies still sell it (see the Appendix).

Interest in making tetraploid conversions has also lessened because of the large number of excellent diploids that are now available. So much progress has been made with them that it is impossible for most of us to guess simply by looking whether a daylily is a diploid or tetraploid.

Understanding Hybridization

Before you collect parent plants and begin to hybridize daylilies in a serious way, learn all you can about the process. Visit other breeders if possible, and explore display gardens that feature new introductions. Join the American Hemerocallis Society, study issues of the *Daylily Journal*, and order the Society's two booklets, *The Art of Hybridizing* and *Some Basic Hemerocallis Genetics* (see the Appendix).

If you have enough space, try to locate your hybridizing bed in an out-of-the-way place where visitors won't easily find it.

Fastidious gardeners often feel they must "neaten up" every flower bed they visit and may, without thinking, pick off the faded blooms you have just pollinated or even the messy-looking seedpods that are forming. This habit, to "neaten up," is so ingrained in some of us that, on more than one occasion, we have absentmindedly picked off some of our own pollinated blossoms. Another reason for isolating your hybridizing bed is that visitors, also without realizing it, sometimes pollinate flowers for you. Many of our customers, seeking out fragrant daylilies, sniff at each one and move pollen about at an alarming rate. Every time we see anyone leaving our fields with a yellowish nose we know that numerous seedpods will be forming where they have traveled. Although we sometimes save the seeds and plant them, we have no idea who the daddy of each one might be.

Be sure the soil in the growing bed for your parent stock is in excellent condition so the plants will thrive and quickly produce well-filled pods of viable seed. At the same time, be careful not to overfertilize these special plants, because if they are growing too vigorously, they may produce an abundance of foliage rather than the blooms and seeds you want.

Certain hereditary characteristics tend to dominate when two plants are cross-pollinated, because both dominant and recessive genes exist in plants, just as in humans and other animals. The characteristic of early bloom, for example, tends to be recessive, and when an early-blooming plant is crossed with a midseason or late-blooming type, most of the offspring are not likely to be early bloomers. Even when two parents that bloom exceptionally early are mated, there may be only a few early-flowering descendants among many seedlings. Fragrance in daylilies is another elusive characteristic, and you've probably noticed that very few of the best cultivars are truly fragrant.

Among the genes that are dominant are those of "eyed" daylilies. By crossing two "eyed" cultivars you are likely to get a good percentage of seedlings with halos or contrasting eyes. Crossing two doubles may result in about half of the offspring being consistently double. Other descendants are likely to produce both single and double flowers on the same plant.

Since not a great deal is known about recessive and dominant genes in daylilies, hybridizers must work with limited information and determine their programs mostly by observing the results. To capture the qualities of the less-dominant genes in a new cultivar, breeders do not always discard their inferior, first-generation seedlings but, instead, keep them for breeding the next generation. Then, according to Mendel's law, the desired traits may show up.

Choosing Parent Stock

When you begin to hybridize, it is best to pick parent daylilies that have been developed in climates similar to your own so the offspring will be acclimated. Choose the best cultivars you can find for your breeding program, thus taking advantage of the work that has already been done. Buy parent plants that have been developed by several different breeders, on the assumption that any one hybridizer may have already exhausted all of the potential from his or her own group of plants.

To obtain the genes you want, it is often necessary to choose a parent that may have an undesirable characteristic. Avoid choosing two parents with similar weaknesses, such as weak petal structure or low bud count, even if they both rate high on the fragrance and flower size you want.

Of the thousands of daylily cultivars in existence, many are fertile in two ways — they produce viable pollen themselves that can be used to fertilize other plants, and they accept viable pollen from other plants which they are able to use to produce seeds. A few are unable to generate viable pollen, but can accept it from other plants and make seeds, so only act as "pod parents." Still others can produce viable pollen, but are unable to accept it from another flower and thus act as "pollen parents." A limited number of cultivars are completely sterile and unable to either produce or accept pollen.

The fertility situation is further complicated by the fact that some daylilies do not act the same when grown in different climates, and their habits may also vary depending on the weather.

Some plants that are described as sterile may not always be completely so. If enough crosses are attempted between supposedly incompatible mates, a few seeds may eventually result. A. B. Stout, the master *Hemerocallis* breeder, is said to have tried 7,135 pollination attempts with 'Europa' before finally producing twenty-three seedpods and seventy seeds. Unfortunately, there is no master listing of which daylilies are fertile in one way or the other, but writers in *The Daylily Journal* frequently report their findings, and one can also often pick up that kind of information by attending daylily conventions and meetings.

There are so many potentially good daylily parents available that we would not attempt to recommend all the cultivars that could possibly lead to success in a breeding program. A beginning hybridizer working toward a certain color has many choices. For example, good red offspring might be produced by using either 'Ed Murray' or 'Mavis Smith' as a parent, and blue offspring by using purple and bluish cultivars such as 'Little Grapette', 'Mood Indigo', 'Prairie Blue Eyes', or 'Grape Velvet'. Some white fanciers use 'Gentle Shepherd', 'Guardian Angel', 'Hope Diamond', 'Joan Senior', 'Call to Remembrance', and 'White Fantasy'; and 'Fairy Tale Pink' is currently a popular pink parent.

Breeders seeking cultivars that bloom over a long season favor 'Stella de Oro' as a parent. For blooms that last more than a day, 'Pat Mercer' is often used. Breeders searching for ruffles and fancy edgings sometimes use 'Dance Ballerina Dance', 'Strawberry Rose', or 'Fairy Tale Pink'.

Those looking for fragrance may choose 'Janet Gayle', 'Hudson Valley', or old-timers such as the Lemon Daylily or 'Hyperion'.

Anyone who likes to play with miniatures has many potential parents from which to choose; in addition to 'Stella de Oro', they include 'Decatur Imp', 'Little Cameo', 'Little Delight', 'Mini Stella', and a host of the Siloams. Daylilies with blotches or halos may be spawned by 'Bandit Man', 'Outrageous', 'Rocket City', 'Radiant Greetings', and again, many of the Siloams.

For the hybridizer seeking the largest possible blooms, certain yellows seem to be prime choices; some of the best are 'Hudson Valley', 'Prairie Moonlight', and 'Susan Elizabeth'. 'Kindly Light', 'Scorpio', and 'Stoplight' are popular with those seeking better spider types.

These recommendations are, of course, only a small number of the excellent cultivars available, and they do not include many of the terrific evergreens that are so popular with southern hybridizers. For more suggestions, see Chapter 15.

Cross-Pollination

Once you have determined which parent plants you want to use in your experimentation, the fun begins. As most gardeners know, the pollination of a flower occurs when the pollen is moved from the anthers at the tips of the stamens (male organs) to the top of the pistil (female organ). Daylily pollen is generally transmitted by insects, primarily bees, but it can also be carried a short distance by the wind. Fertilization begins when the pollen adheres to the sticky stigma at the top of the pistil. The pollen grains go down the hollow pistil where they meet the ovules, and fertilization takes place. If all goes well, the fertilized eggs develop into embryos that mature to form seeds. One pollen grain is necessary for the formation of each seed.

In most of the species daylilies and many early hybrids, the pistil is short enough to be easily brushed with pollen as the bees, in the process of gathering nectar in the throat, enter and leave the trumpet-shaped blooms. For this reason, the early daylilies often developed many seedpods. The blooms of modern daylilies are flatter in shape, so their long pistil sticks out well beyond the petals; this design makes it less likely that insects will touch it in their nectar-seeking travels. Consequently, most of the new cultivars seldom produce seed unless they are pollinated by hand, which works to the advantage of hybridizers because accidental pollination becomes far less likely.

Unfortunately, the hard-working bees often mix the pollen from the stamens of one daylily with the pollen on another plant's stamens even though they don't come into contact with the pistil. Therefore, it is best to do all hand-pollination on a dry, sunny day as early in the morning as the flowers open, before the bees have a chance to "pollute" the pollen you plan to use.

Pollen can be transferred with a small brush, but because brushes are difficult to clean between uses, hybridizers often use cotton swabs instead, employing a new one for each cross in order to avoid mixing the pollen. It is also possible to simply remove one of the six stamens from the male (pollen parent), and dust its pollen onto the top of the pistil of the receiving, female blossom (pod parent). The best results come from gathering the pollen when it is fresh, soon after the flowers open, even if you plan to save it for later use. When pollen becomes a whitish color later in the day, it is less viable; it is also less viable during hot weather.

Many hybridizers place a bag over the flower for a few hours after they have pollinated it to prevent unwanted pollen from

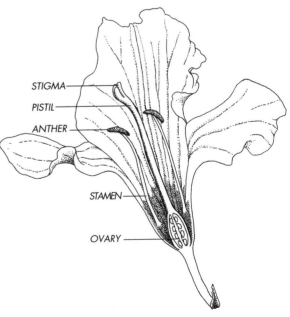

STIGMA

PISTIL

ANTHER

STAMEN

OVARY

CROSS-SECTION OF A DAYLILY FLOWER

adhering to the pistil and competing with the selected parent's pollen before it has had a chance to work. The purity of the pollen is extremely important in a controlled experiment, and some hybridizers are so anxious to get fresh, uncontaminated pollen that they force open the buds a bit before nature is ready.

Some also recommend covering the buds of both parents with plastic bags the night before the blooms to be crossed open, so that both the pollen and the pistil that will receive it are certain to be uncontaminated until the hybridizer is ready. The bags also keep the flowers and pollen dry in case of rain or a heavy dew.

Unless a plant is quite vigorous, or you desperately need a lot of seed from that particular cultivar, it is best not to allow more than one seedpod to set on each scape even if you pollinate several flowers. If the plant seems at all weak, one pod per plant may be enough. It consumes a lot of the plant's energy to produce a pod full of seeds, and you don't want it to be at the expense of future plant growth and blooms. Also, to conserve energy, we pick off all the remaining buds on a scape after a seedpod has started to form, so the plant's strength will go into developing the seeds rather than into producing new blossoms.

Don't expect 100 percent success with your pollination. Some people estimate that pods form in only 40 percent of the crosses made, even when every precaution is taken. Take this into consideration and always pollinate more blooms than you need.

Storing Pollen

You may occasionally want to cross-pollinate two cultivars that do not blossom at the same time, or "borrow" pollen from a friend who lives far away. Pollen can be safely stored for some time if it is kept cool and dry. Many hybridizers brush it into empty gelatin capsules and seal them tightly. Others store cotton swabs that have been dusted with pollen and cut to the right size so they fit into tight, plastic 35mm film containers. Still other hybridizers pick and store the anthers (the tips of the stamens). If you choose to do the latter, do not include any of the stem of the stamen, because it will add moisture and spoil the pollen in a short time.

Label each gelatin capsule or small container, and put it in a tight jar with some silica or other drying agent to absorb any moisture. When pollen is kept sealed and dry, it will last for a week unrefrigerated. Refrigerated, it usually stays viable for the entire hybridizing season; when frozen, it should keep for a year.

When using the stored pollen, the pistil can be dipped into the gelatin capsules, or dusted from the cotton swabs. Be sure to keep the pollen storage container out of the sun at all times when you are using it. A pasteboard box makes a nice shade.

Since it takes eight to ten weeks for daylily seeds to mature fully, it is best to pollinate the first blooms that open on the cultivars you want to cross, rather than waiting until later in the season. Hybridizers in the North, even when they pollinate early, often experience problems in getting the seedpods to ripen completely, and it is especially difficult to get the late-blooming cultivars to mature at all. Some northern breeders cover their mother plants at the first sign of frost; others keep them in large pots that can be moved into a greenhouse when cool weather begins.

Another trick sometimes used to extend the ripening period is to remove the scapes with the immature seedpods and place them in a vase of water with a small amount of sugar in it. Keep this in a warm place, cut off a bit of stem each week to ensure the scape's continuous absorption of the solution, and change the solution at least every three weeks until the pod ripens.

Daylily seedpods vary in size, but most are usually about the size of a small pecan, and each contains about a dozen seeds. They are ripe as soon as the pods turn dark brown. Most growers prefer to let the seeds ripen completely on the plant, if climatic conditions permit it. This means that you must allow the pods to stay on the scapes long enough to become sufficiently dry so the seeds rattle around inside but still gather them before the pods open and spill their seeds. Usually a pod cracks open at the top a few days before it splits open entirely, so watch the pods carefully. They are not likely to open on a rainy or cold day.

When you harvest the seeds before the pods have opened naturally, it is likely that the seeds will not be completely dry. If you intend to plant them immediately, there is no need for further drying. But if you are going to store them, spread the seeds on a screen for a few days of additional drying after removing them from the pod, because excess moisture will cause them to rot in storage.

Some seed savers advocate picking the pods early anyway, as soon as they begin to turn color but before they have dried completely. If you do this, complete the drying process in a warm, airy place, spreading out the pods on an elevated window screen or something similar. Let them dry until the pods crack. Then open them and dry the seeds a bit more if they are going to be stored. Don't forget them and allow them to dry for weeks, however, or they may not have enough vitality left to germinate.

For further directions about planting and growing seeds, see Chapter 9.

One of the tough things to do when you are under the pressure of hybridizing and gardening is to remember to label everything carefully — the breeding stock, the pollen, if you save it, and of course, the seeds and new seedlings. Only by keeping excellent records can you follow the progress of each cross and work toward whatever plant characteristics you have in mind (see page 120).

After you pollinate a plant, fasten a label at the base of the bloom that gives its pedigree. A typical notation might read, "7-2-91 Mulberry Ripple X Sdlg. 396." This indicates the date of the cross, then the name of the mother plant (the one receiving the pollen), followed by an X and then the name of the father plant (the one donating the pollen). If more than one cross is being made between the same parents, indicate also the number of the cross. All this information and anything else of interest should also be recorded in your breeding program notebook. These records follow the seeds from the time you place them into containers, through the seeding and transplant stage, and finally through the years you are evaluating all their good and bad characteristics.

Whenever you discover a quality seed-

After you hand-pollinate a plant, fasten a label at the base of the bloom that gives its pedigree. This tag shows the date of the cross, the name of the mother plant (receives the pollen) followed by an X ("crossed with") and then the name of the father plant (donates the pollen). The number indicates the number of the cross between these two parents.

ling, assign it a new designation or number so it can be identified for possible introduction or for use in hybridizing more promising seedlings. Those that don't measure up to your standards can be given away, moved into a suitable flower bed, or discarded.

The numbered seedlings you have selected for future breeding (called F_1) can be used either for *line crossing* (crossing of the most promising of the new plants that originated from the seeds of the same parents) or *back crossing* (crossing seedlings with one of their parents) or *out crossing* (crossing seedlings with completely unrelated cultivars). Succeeding *filial* generations of seedlings are designated F_2, F_3, etc.

Patience, we have found, is extremely necessary in the evaluation process of a new seedling. Although sometimes you know right away that a plant is not worth bothering with further, it is not always the last word when a seedling shows promise the first year. Many times we were very excited about a first bloom, only to find that most of the flowers that followed were quite inferior. One "first" blossom we had last year was a full, huge, gorgeous double yellow, but all those that followed it were small and single. The same inconsistency can be true of other plant characteristics. Sometimes a plant is not spectacular the first year or two but eventually turns out to be a winner when it reaches its full potential. Although some seedlings can be discarded at once as hopeless, successful breeders do not hurry to either name or throw away plants after their first- and second-year blooms. As with friends, it may take several years to know for sure what they are really like.

To evaluate seedlings properly takes considerable skill and experience, but the AHS *Daylily Judges' Handbook* can help you measure their characteristics. The handbook defines what is meant by good color, form, texture, and substance in flowers, and what is meant by proper scape relationships, good branching, and bud count. Talk with other breeders, too, to learn what procedures they use and how many years they allow for the process.

Registering New Cultivars

It is not a good idea to register and introduce a new daylily unless you are positive that you have one that is truly superior and unusual. It isn't doing the daylily world a favor to introduce a plant that is much like others already being grown, or one that is not truly outstanding.

Another caveat about seedling development: When you have discovered a nice seedling that you don't intend to register, be careful not to give it a name, especially if you intend to give it, or its divisions, away. Chances are that the name you choose will already be in use, and as your friends pass their misnamed plants on to others, you will have helped to confuse daylily nomenclature even more than it is already.

While you are in the process of evaluating what appears to be a seedling worthy of registration, it's a good idea to propagate a few divisions and grow them in several different places, perhaps even sharing a few with friends. Then if you lose your original clump by accident, there will still be some left to propagate.

When you are ready to register your new origination, write to the American Hemerocallis Society (see Appendix) for the necessary forms. The society is recognized by the International Horticultural Congress and operates under the International Code of Nomenclature for Cultivated Plants. The forms require the following information:

1. The name you have chosen. If the name describes the plant in any way, it must be honest; it is important that the name does not deceive the public. The name must also be one not registered previously, and it must meet the requirements listed later in this chapter.
2. Height of scape in inches as it grows in your garden.
3. Season of bloom, whether early, midseason, or late. You should also state if it is a rebloomer.
4. Diameter of the flower in inches.
5. Color described briefly. Registering does not require the terms listed in the Color Dictionary.
6. Blooming habits: whether it is a day bloomer or a night bloomer, and whether or not it is an extended bloomer.
7. Foliage: dormant, semi-evergreen, or evergreen.
8. Whether it is diploid or tetraploid.
9. Whether it has single or double blooms.

10. Name of the originator or originators, and the registrant if different from the originator. Also complete addresses.

11. Other information such as parentage can be included to become part of the record, even though it is not required.

12. Registration fee.

When the completed form is received and approved, the cultivar is officially named and registered, and the information will be included in the next Hemerocallis Check List. (See Appendix for information on ordering these lists.)

Introducing Your New Plant

Although introduction is not required for registration, this step is a logical one, and it can be done by the originator or by a commercial nursery. To introduce a new cultivar, it must be offered for sale to the public in a printed or mechanically duplicated, dated price list, magazine, or other publication; and the person, or firm, selling the plant is the official "introducer." All introducers should send copies of their catalog, price list, or publication offering the new introduction to the Registrar of the American Hemerocallis Society.

This information becomes part of the registering record and will be included in the Hemerocallis Check List. The cultivar also becomes eligible for the awards and honors of the American Hemerocallis Society, should one choose to compete.

Naming Plants

Coming up with a different name for your wonderful new plant is not easy anymore. We have often thought that many cultivars, such as 'Breakaway' and 'Pretty Please', were named after race horses. Pauline Henry, a hybridizer in Missouri, creates original names for her cultivars by prefixing Siloam, the town where she lives, to each one. Descriptive names are hard to come by because most have already been used, and the society has firm rules about naming plants (see page 119). Unless you are absolutely sure your name has never been used, check each of the directories that list all the names that have been registered over the years with the American Hemerocallis Society (see Appendix).

If making money from your new creation figures into your plans, you need to give even more thought to its naming. At our nursery we are aware that the name, rather than its other attributes, often sells the plant. 'Dance Ballerina Dance' and 'Fairy Tale Pink' appeal more to prospective buyers than would 'Summer Compost' or 'Benedict Arnold'. Some people seem to feel that if a daylily is named after a person, it must be a special plant to rate such an honor. The cultivar 'Frans Hals' creates interest because of its association with the artist, and 'Bette Davis Eyes' triggers all sorts of images. We have had people choose 'Sugar Candy' or 'Little Rainbow' simply because the name appealed to them.

Regulations about Naming Daylily Cultivars

From the booklet *Daylilies, Everything You Always Wanted to Know about Daylilies*, published by the American Hemerocallis Society.

1. The name of a cultivar should be a common and well-understood word or words, preferably in the English language, although well-known words or phrases or recognized transliterations from other languages may be used. Personal names must not be translated. Do not use Latin or Greek words, since these are for botanical use only.

2. The name should consist of one or two words but not more than three words.

3. The accidental or intentional misspelling of any word having a recognized spelling or usage is not acceptable unless it is the actual spelling of a person's name. Example: Daylight, not Daylite.

4. A slight variation in the spelling of another name is not acceptable. Example: Gold Nugget and Golden Nuggett.

5. Names that are likely to be confused with existing names must be avoided. Example: Beatrice and Beatrix.

6. Avoid names containing abbreviations, initials, numerals, symbols, apostrophes, accents, commas, hyphens, or any other marks likely to be misplaced or omitted. Avoid as a prefix to a name the articles *a* and *the* and their equivalents, unless required by linguistic customs.

7. Avoid descriptive terms that apply to characteristics not exclusive or potentially exclusive to one particular cultivar. Examples: Ruffled Petals and Green Throat.

8. Avoid names that exaggerate the merits of a cultivar or which may become inaccurate through the introduction of new cultivars. Examples: Earliest of All and Latest of All.

9. Names containing forms of address are not acceptable. Examples: Miss, Mrs., Mister, Doctor, and their equivalents in other languages.

10. The use of the surname of the originator or introducer as a part of a name is not permissible, except where such surnames are better known as a noun or adjective. Example: Robert Brown could register Brown Moth, but not Brown's Choice.

11. The legal or professional name of a living person can be used as a name for a *Hemerocallis* cultivar only when written permission is given by the person concerned.

12. A two- or three-word name in use as a *Hemerocallis* cultivar name cannot be reversed or rearranged and used for another cultivar. Example: Pink Diamond and Diamond Pink.

13. Individuals or groups wishing to name a cultivar other than their own origination must have the written permission of the originator.

What does it take to be a successful hybridizer? Some breeders consistently turn out winners, while others labor for decades with little to show. Most originators would tell you modestly that they have been lucky, but if you watch them operate, you soon realize that luck is not the only reason they are successful. Most have full-time jobs and devote only part of their time to hybridizing, but they are extremely dedicated to their hobby. As one breeder said, "We eat, work, and dream daylilies." We who merely grow them should feel a great sense of gratitude as we enjoy the results of their labors.

Those of us who are less scientific in our hybridizing programs, still have a lot of fun moving the pollen from flower to flower. It is exciting to watch the first buds develop on a new seedling, and if there is going to be only one bloom on the new plant the first year, we plan to be around to see it on the day it opens. We enjoy the surprises that appear throughout the season and always find it difficult to throw away the plants that are almost, but not quite, good enough to move into the flower bed.

We hope you will try hybridizing, too, and wish you the best of luck.

DAYLILY BREEDING RECORD

Seedling Number_____ Tetraploid____ Diploid_____ Foliage_____
Pod Parent_____ Pollen Parent_____
Date Pollinated_____ Date Planted_____ Transplanted_____

— **EVALUATION INFORMATION** —

FIRST YEAR
Date of First bloom_____ Last Bloom_____
Comments_____

SECOND YEAR
Date of First Bloom_____ Last Bloom_____
Comments_____

Branching_____ Bud Count_____ Fragrance_____
Foliage type_____ Nocturnal_____ Rebloomer_____
Bud builder_____ Vigor_____

(subsequent evaluation on reverse side)

Keep track of your hybridizing experiments by devising a file card on which to record parentage, important dates, and your own evaluation.

CHAPTER 11

Arranging Daylilies

EACH JULY for the past thirty years the small community of Dighton, Massachusetts, has hosted a popular daylily show in their historic church, where worship services have been held since 1770. First suggested by our friends Wayne and Flora Philbrook, this one-day event involves local garden clubs, junior garden clubs, children, growers, and individuals who vie with each other to produce an extravaganza of *Hemerocallis* arrangements that fill the church with a different theme each year. The participants have been challenged by such themes as "A Boston Tea Party," "Symphony of Flowers," "Grandmother's Memories," and "Lilies around the World."

The Dighton event is only one of many daylily shows around North America each summer. It has no affiliation with the American Hemerocallis Society, but many regional groups of the AHS sponsor annual shows; and the national AHS then awards a rotating trophy, the Mabel Y. Yaste Award, to the most outstanding arrangement among all the winners of accredited regional shows.

A daylily exhibit is unique among flower shows because, unlike an ordinary show when the arrangements can be created the day before, the blooms must be picked and arranged on the very morning of the exhibition, unless, of course, buds are picked the previous evening. One might think that all the work would hardly be worth the trouble, considering the brief lifespan of each bloom, but both exhibitors and viewers look forward to these events, and the memory of their beauty is anything but ephemeral.

In spite of their short lives, daylily blooms have always given arrangers (and their viewers) a great deal of pleasure, whether they simply position one single striking blossom in a Japanese Ikebana line arrangement, or create a massive, colorful bouquet typical of those of eighteenth-century Williamsburg. The stunning new cultivars that began to appear in the 1950s and

1960s stimulated even more use of daylilies in arrangements, both at home and in shows. They have become far too beautiful to enjoy only in the garden.

There are obvious drawbacks to using daylilies for your arrangements. One is the last-minute timing, since you cannot gather the blossoms a week, or even a day ahead, and store them in the refrigerator or a cool basement as you might peonies or chrysanthemums. Also, although daylilies make an ideal centerpiece for summer luncheons, they are not a good choice for a late dinner party. One woman, whose guests lingered over their dessert, told of watching in horror as one daylily bloom after another quietly folded before their eyes.

We recall sitting through a dance recital one summer evening with one eye on the dancers and the other on a large bouquet of daylilies we had supplied as decoration for the performance. We were hoping that the final pirouettes and bows would be over before the beautiful flowers took their own exit. Fortunately, the applause faded before the daylilies did, but we were taking a calculated risk. One lady even asked if she could use the arrangement for an event she had planned for the next day! We had to confess that she probably would not find it as attractive in the morning.

If you want to feel secure that your arrangement will not turn into a bedraggled "pumpkin," like Cinderella's coach, use extended-blooming daylily cultivars that stay open after darkness falls, or those that open in the late afternoon or early evening.

You can also condition daylilies that open in the morning to last throughout the evening. The American Hemerocallis Society recommends that on the night before you want the arrangement, cut the scapes that have buds you are sure will open the following day. Place them in the refrigerator and, a few hours before you intend to arrange them, take them out and let the blooms open in strong incandescent lighting. The daylilies will be fooled into thinking their day is just beginning. Another way to make daylilies last through the evening is to cut them in the morning just as they are opening and refrigerate them. Then, in the early evening, take them out and arrange them. With either method it is a good idea to experiment in advance with the cultivars you are using, to be sure they will react in the way you anticipate to the cold and light conditions.

Once you have acknowledged the drawbacks of the daylily's lifespan, you will find that there are advantages to it, too. With minor adjustments, an arrangement can last for many days and provide a daily change of bloom. The second day, when the first day's blossoms have faded, new ones open if the scapes you picked had plenty of buds. Lovely new flowers emerge each day to keep the arrangement going and provide a daily surprise. It is necessary to remove the faded blooms each morning, of course, and to turn a bloom here and there to face the proper direction. You may also need to add a few newly picked scapes with blooms to fill in the bare spots. But this "revision" process takes little effort and each bouquet will hold for at least three to five days.

When you have spent some time with daylilies, you will easily recognize, in a stroll around the garden, which buds will be opening the following day. Arrangers sometimes pick scapes with ready-to-burst buds the night before they want the bouquet. Rev. Wayne Philbrook sometimes took such scapes on his hospital calls in order to provide a colorful morning surprise to a patient who had been given a green bouquet the previous evening.

The fact that the blooms last nearly as long out of water as they do in makes them very versatile. We have seen small, ruffled cultivars wired together with a bit of baby's-breath and a ribbon in an attractive corsage, for example, and no orchids ever looked better. Remove the stamens from any daylily bloom used in a corsage, because the pollen stains clothing, and the stain is difficult to remove. It may be advisable, also, to remove the stamens from flowers used in arrangements if there is danger of the pollen dropping on linens or brushing against walls. Pollen stains can be distressing, but we have found that they can be removed by using a commercial pre-wash stain remover. Be careful not to rub or smudge the pollen first. It is a tenacious substance.

Katherine Noble Cutler, in her fine book *Flower Arranging for All Occasions* (Doubleday, 1981), tells of wiring single blooms to a florist's pick and inserting each into a long-lasting background arrangement of greenery such as euonymous or laurel. Each day she removed the faded blooms and added a new assortment, varying the colors, style, and number of blossoms, to keep her arrangement going for weeks without becoming boring.

We have used daylilies for a hastily arranged centerpiece by simply gathering a

An informal arrangement of several different colors and cultivars of daylilies looks best if the plant material is at least 1½ times the height of the container.

dozen beautiful blooms and placing them in a pile in the center of a table.

Picking the Flowers

The ideal time to pick daylilies is in the morning soon after they have opened so they will be fresh and undamaged by wind or insects. To collect the scapes we use a large plastic utility pail with a few inches of water in the bottom for ballast as well as for moisture. We transport a maximum of a dozen or so scapes at a time because many of the petals are so delicate and fragile they cannot touch each other and must be handled as if they were thin glass.

Daylily arrangers have concocted a few tricks to help bring out the best in their flowers. Some always water the plants heavily for three or four days before picking the scapes if it doesn't rain, so the flowers will be well supplied with moisture. This extra water not only increases the bloom size, but it tends to improve the petal weight and substance as well.

Many red cultivars spot badly from dew or rain and look as if they have been afflicted with white measles, so on the night before the blooms are to be picked, some arrangers cover the buds of those that will open the following day. If you do this, be sure to use a bag that is large enough for the flower to open fully, and remove it just as soon as the dew evaporates in the morning. Perfectionists also pick off any large buds that are close to the buds of the flowers they plan to use, if they feel they might prevent a prize-winning specimen from opening completely.

Containers

The container and its relationship to the flowers it holds can make or break the effect of a bouquet. Just as good landscaping should complement, but not distract from, a home, the container should act as a background for the flowers rather than the focal point.

With daylilies you have a great deal of latitude in choosing the proper container. We sometimes position a single, elegant scape in a slim crystal vase, yet each summer we also arrange at least one huge bouquet of numerous varieties in a large, wooden, Revolutionary War powder keg. Containers with a matte finish and subdued earth-toned colors are more suitable for most arrangements than those with bright, shiny exteriors that clash or compete with the flowers. Baskets, now available in so many sizes and shapes, lend themselves particularly well as containers, especially for an informal arrangement. They can be filled with graceful greens in a suitable lined container, and from day to day you can change the daylilies to suit your mood, sometimes from one complete color scheme to another.

Arranging

We know people who never arrange their flowers, on the theory that the blooms are lovely enough to speak for themselves. "Arrangements are unnatural looking," they contend. It is true that a poorly constructed arrangement can make flowers appear unnatural, but it is much more likely that when bloom-laden scapes are plopped casually into a milk bottle or pitcher, the effect will be even more unnatural. With just a bit of care and a few tricks, it is easy to give nature a hand and create a lovely bouquet.

If you are arranging for competition in a flower show, it is important to study the schedule for the show in advance and decide which artistic divisions or classes you wish to enter. Before the day of the show you should have your idea firmly in mind and prepare the container and any accessories you may need to use as background. The greenery and other plant materials can also be arranged in advance, but the daylilies must be picked the morning of the show. Most people prefer to assemble daylilies on the site rather than risk breakage or misalignment of the flowers en route. When you do this, be sure that the containers you use for transporting the scapes are heavily weighted with pebbles or water, so they won't fall over when the vehicle takes a sharp corner. Take along several additional scapes, as well, to be sure you'll have enough.

Rules for arrangements in flower shows are precise, and you should find out what the judges will be looking for before you enter so you will not be marked down for some simple failure of "mechanics." The suggestions that follow may not prepare you to compete in a "judged" show, but we hope they will help you use your daylilies creatively at home as well as for church, summer weddings, birthdays, and other special events.

Before you begin to arrange, and even before you pick the flowers or choose a container, look carefully at the place the arrangement will be. The location will guide you to select the proper size and shape of the bouquet, as well as its colors.

Some sort of greenery is essential in most arrangements to provide a background for the daylilies. Since the scapes have no foliage, you must pick it from the clump of daylilies or get it from another plant. One of the easiest and most satisfactory arrangements for a busy gardener is to place half a dozen favorite blooms in a shallow dish with a few hosta leaves, which offer many varieties in shades of green; their bold shape and texture is a pleasing foil for the daylilies. For most bouquets we prefer greens with mass, rather than the thin, sword-shaped daylily foliage. In addition to hosta, the foliage of peonies or viburnum, with its attractive berries, fills the bill nicely. We occasionally use evergreens such as arborvitae or even needled varieties such as fir or hemlock. Ferns or the foliage of roses, blueberries, and many other plants can also be effective as a background for daylilies.

Other perennials with contrasting textures and shapes add spice to a daylily arrangement, and each arranger has favorites. We feel that the cobalt-blue flowers of globe thistle *(Echinops)* complement the vivid daylily colors very well, and one of our friends swears by the lavender-blue flowers of *Hosta ventricosa* in her daylily bouquets. We also like the flat-topped *Achillea* 'Coronation Gold', as well as delphinium, phlox, and Shasta daisy in their seasons. Country roadsides furnish many lovely wildflowers that go well with daylilies, including Queen-Anne's-lace, black-eyed Susan, and common goldenrod.

Daylily scapes are so tall that it is easy to get just exactly the height you want by clipping. Bouquets for a buffet, mantle, or stand can be taller than those for a table centerpiece, which must be low enough for guests to easily see over it. For the best proportion, the plant material should be approximately 1½ times the height of a tall container, and 1½ times the width of a short one. Such rules are made to be broken, of course, but it is important to keep proportion in mind.

Although many different materials can be used to make the stiff daylily scapes stay precisely where you want them, we prefer the instant Oasis that is available from most garden centers and florist shops. Cut a piece of Oasis so that it will fit firmly into the container, or implant a cube of it onto a large pinholder that has been covered with a piece of nylon stocking (for ease of removal) and attached to the container with florist's clay. Then soak the block thoroughly in water and begin to arrange. Insert the greenery first to cover the block of Oasis and form the background; then add the scapes and other plant materials.

When we have only a single scape of a particularly beautiful new daylily, we hesitate to sacrifice all the forming buds in an arrangement, so we pluck a single bloom and float it in a dish of water, like a water lily, on our dining room table. We never feel guilty about picking a gorgeous bloom when we don't disturb the whole scape. There will be new ones out the next day.

It is not necessary to be a Monet or Van Gogh to arrange daylilies beautifully. Examine other bouquets that you like, notice how they are composed, and experiment. If you have doubts about your ability or want to enter competition in a show, it is helpful to read a book on arranging that explains the basics of good design and such principles as form, texture, scale, color, and balance. Balance is particularly important when you're working with daylilies because many of them are so large that arrangements can easily appear to be top-heavy or lopsided. To avoid an unbalanced bouquet, use smaller, "lighter" blossoms, buds, or other flowers at the top, and larger blooms near the center and the base. An arrangement is better balanced, too, when you position "heavy" dark colors such as deep red, rust, and near black in the center of the arrangement and the lighter, more airy shades around the edges.

Obviously, the colors you choose should not clash with each other in the arrangement, or with the colors in the room. Bright pink and vivid orange can be beautiful in a border when they are separated by other more muted shades, but in an indoor setting the colors are likely to ruin the effect of the entire bouquet.

CHAPTER 12

Preserving Your Daylilies on Film

YOU CAN SPOT a dedicated *Hemerocallis* lover by the camera or camcorder he or she is toting while making the rounds of daylily gardens during the blooming season. In their vast array of colors and shapes, daylilies are extraordinarily photogenic, and both amateur and professional camera bugs enjoy making them last longer than a day. We honest-to-gosh Hemerocalliphiles want to enjoy our beautiful flowers all year long.

Like many other photographers, both amateur and professional, we use a single lens reflex 35mm camera for our daylily photos. It is relatively lightweight to carry around, easily fitted with a close-up lens, and allows us to take transparencies (slides) for presentations to garden clubs as well as high-quality prints for albums.

It is important to be thoroughly familiar with the camera equipment you choose and to know exactly what it is and is not capable of doing. Experts get far better pictures with cheap cameras than less knowledgeable

photographers with very expensive ones.

The best type of film for plant photography is a matter of individual preference. Since color film is usually preferable to black and white for plants, it is what we will discuss here. If you intend to enlarge photos for exhibition or sell them for reproduction in magazines, use slide film to take transparencies rather than prints, since for the printing process, it is easier to separate the various colors in transparencies. Ektachrome film is excellent to emphasize vivid greenery and blue sky; Kodachrome is best to capture vivid oranges, reds, and yellows. It is very difficult, with any film, to record authentic shades of purple and violet.

In general, the slower the film speed, the sharper the image, the more accurate the color, and the finer the grain, which is an important consideration if you intend to enlarge the photograph. The proper speed of film can keep a discussion between photographers going for hours. Kodachrome

25, Kodachrome 64, or Ektachrome 64 Professional Film are all excellent for slides, although the professional film is somewhat temperamental and must be refrigerated. For prints, Kodak Ektar 25 or Kodacolor 100 are both exceptional and widely used. Last summer we used both types of print film in taking hundreds of daylily photos for a display album and found little difference in the quality, but they were enlarged only to standard print size. The Ektar 25 would undoubtedly have produced a sharper image if we had enlarged them. Many photographers also use various imported films.

Additional equipment for taking good plant photos is optional. If your camera doesn't handle close-ups, you will probably want a close-up lens or a zoom lens with a macro setting. A tripod is useful for low-light situations and to hold the camera steady if you have trouble with camera "shake," but it is usually unnecessary unless you need to photograph with a shutter speed of less than $\frac{1}{125}$. A light meter of some sort is essential if you are to get good photos, and most good cameras have one that is already built in. When precision is important, however, photographers carry an independent meter to double-check the light reading. Some use filters of various kinds for special effects, but filters change the colors, so if you use them be aware of what each type does.

As you become more professional and particular, other accessories you may want to use include a light reflector, such as a piece of cardboard covered with aluminum foil, to help direct the light into dark places, or a light diffuser to help reduce glaring sunlight. Some people carry a sheet of opaque plastic to use as a windbreak, but we find that if we are patient, even on our windy hilltop, the breezes stop to rest occasionally.

A large garden filled with colorful daylily cultivars in full bloom is a breathtaking sight. It is also, we have discovered, a sight that is extremely difficult to capture accurately on film. For years we have photographed such gardens or large fields of daylilies, only to have the photos record a view that is disappointingly flat and washed out, not at all what we thought we saw in the viewfinder.

Much of our problem has been too much light; we tend to take such photos in the middle of a beautiful sunny day, and the camera records the glare and the shadows. When photographing many flowers or a large garden, the morning hours from 6 to 10 A.M. are best because the light is "softer" then. We cannot always photograph our daylilies then because, unlike in more southern climates, many do not fully open until after 10 A.M. on cool summer mornings. Fortunately, late afternoon, when the lighting is again subdued, also works quite well; the lighting effects often seem even more dramatic than in the morning. Some photographers who need to take photos in the morning or evening use a flash and report that the color in many shots is better than in natural lighting.

On the other hand, the middle of the

day is the best time to take close-up photos of individual daylily blooms because films are balanced for mid-day lighting. The actual flower colors show up most accurately, experts say, when the photo is taken from approximately 10 A.M. to 3 P.M.

If you have a choice of weather in which to record your daylilies, choose a bright, overcast day without direct sunlight, which casts contrasting shadows. If the day is rather dark, you could use a flash for close-ups to better control the lighting.

Depth of field refers to the range that is sharply focused in front and in back of the subject of the photograph. To achieve a depth of field that is as deep as possible, it is necessary to keep the lens aperture small (depth of field becomes shorter, the more you open the lens). A high f-stop, therefore, either $f/11$, $f/16$ or $f/22$, is preferable for close-up photographs. Of course, the shutter speed must then be adjusted accordingly to a slower speed, depending on the amount of light available.

Individual Close-ups

When you are shooting a series of close-up photos of different, individual daylily cultivars, as we did for the display album that we show our customers, it works well to shoot the photos at the same distance from each flower, so their relative sizes can be compared. One easy way to do this is to set the camera for the shortest possible distance and move it toward or away from the flower until it is in perfect focus. A large bloom

completely fills the frame, but when shooting miniatures you can record several blooms of the same plant in each photo.

Although natural backgrounds are usually most effective, to capture a bloom at its best, you may want to use an artificial, neutral background with no distracting foliage or buds, as you'll find in catalog photos such as those published by Gilbert H. Wild, Inc. You can always hold up a piece of colored posterboard, but if you are taking many shots, it is easier to construct a portable board of plywood or a similar material and either attach colored paper to it or paint it with a nonglossy finish. Black is one of the most effective backgrounds for daylilies.

When you are composing a photograph of an individual daylily, study each one from several angles. Each has a best side, and you probably do not want to record blemishes from a water spot or other imperfections. Pick off all imperfect blooms, buds, or foliage that are obvious in the viewfinder, as well as anything that may be crowding the flower you want. Check, too, to be sure that a bee is not buried deep in the throat, unless you want it there for effect. Some photographers use atomizers to spray water over the blossoms to accentuate the color shadings; or they sprinkle a drop or two of water on a petal to resemble morning dew.

When photographing a long border of daylilies, if you point the camera directly at it and shoot it "head on," the resulting photo is likely to be dull and flat. It is more effective to snap the picture from an angle that leads the viewer into the garden and creates more depth. A spot of color in the foreground — a clump of red daylilies, for example — helps to make the scene more lively. In such a shot, it is usually best to focus on the foreground and let the background blur into the distance, unless you are aiming for special effects.

The number of shots you need to take of each flower or scene depends, of course, on how necessary it is to get a photo of quality. Professional photographers often snap hundreds of photos to get one special shot that is perfect for a book, magazine, advertisement, or display. Most of us don't need that kind of selection, but if you are photographing a potential daylily prize-winner, take several shots at different lens settings and exposures, and if possible, on different days. You may want to *bracket,* that is, make one exposure according to your meter and then make subsequent exposures that are slightly (⅓ to ½ stop) over- and under-exposures from the original setting.

Take a notebook and pen with you into the garden to keep track of the photos you are snapping, because everyone is interested in the names of daylilies. One time we were showing slides to a garden club, and, not wanting to bore the audience with names, we described only flower forms, textures, and types. We soon found out that everyone wanted to know the name of each bloom, and many wrote down their favorites, of those that we could recall. Some photographers place a sign next to the flower, but even a neatly printed one distracts from the plant's beauty. It is better to list numbers in a notebook from 1 to 24 or 1 to 36, depending on the size of your film, and write down the name of each cultivar as you take the photo. It is time-consuming and a bother, but you'll be glad you did it.

Even if you use the best film and camera on a perfect day and shoot the best daylilies in the world with lots of expertise, if you get the film developed and printed at a fast-finish, bargain place, you could be disappointed. If money is a decisive factor, it is far better to take fewer photos and have them processed by a custom laboratory. Even if one-hour processing is tempting, good things are well worth waiting for.

Reproducing Daylily Prints

Both slides and prints can be duplicated by film processors, but if you need extra prints for display purposes, color copiers and print-making machines are available in camera and office supply stores or at printing firms. The quality of color reproduction varies, but it is surprisingly good, and the price becomes lower each year.

Rental Films and Videos

The American Hemerocallis Society maintains a slide and video library, as we mentioned before, and it may be instructive for you to rent a few programs for viewing and notice how others photograph daylilies (see the Appendix for ordering instructions). The programs of 100 slides each cover such topics as "Gardens Old and New," "Gardening with Daylilies," and "AHS Daylily Arrangements — from 1950 to 1980s." Video programs include David Riseman's award-winning 1987 "Visit to Florida Gardens," as well as other garden tours.

The American Hemerocallis Society gives out several awards for daylily photography:

The **A. D. Roquemore Memorial Award** is given for the best 35mm slide showing a complete daylily plant including flower, scape, and foliage.

The **Robert Way Schlumpf Award** is two silver trays, one for the best 35mm slide featuring daylilies in the landscape, and the other for the best 35mm slide of an individual flower.

The **Lazarus Memorial Award** is for the best video presentation relating to daylilies.

Several regional awards are also given.

Daylily Videos

We have found that our camcorder is one of the most effective ways to record our daylilies. With no skill whatsoever we take good shots as we walk around the backyard, then go into the house and view them immediately. If we're not happy with the results, we simply go outdoors and do it over again.

As with prints and slides, long shots of large borders are not as effective as close-ups of a single flower or a clump of flowers, though a good video needs some of both for visual interest. Manual focusing usually gives better results than leaving the camera on automatic focus, but experimentation will soon teach you what works best for you.

Our earliest attempts produced very choppy movements from one scene to the next, but we have learned to leave the camera focused on each bloom long enough so it can be fully appreciated before panning slowly to the next shot in a movement much slower than the eyes would normally turn. We try not to photograph too many similar flowers at one time because it becomes visually boring, but instead, mix flowers of different shades and sizes, as well as those with blotches, ruffles, and contrasting edgings.

A commentary along with the tape adds greatly to its effect. It is best to have two people working on the project so that one can concentrate on the technical part of the photography as the other describes the daylilies. Our attempts to play tape-recorded music in the background have not been successful because we had to stop the camera whenever we moved to the next garden area, and the resulting music was very jerky on the videotape. If your camera allows it, you can dub in music and vocal descriptions later, but it requires an excellent recall of daylily names unless you follow a script.

Action is necessary in a video just as in a movie film, or the daylilies might as well be in a slide show. A slight breeze adds movement to the flowers, and children and pets moving about naturally help to make a film more fun.

When you are filming gardens other than your own, it is both entertaining and useful to record signs or mailboxes, as well as the buildings and an interview with the owner or gardener.

We learn more each year as we tote our cameras around and read books on photography, look at other people's pictures, and talk with skilled photographers. Though our photographs will never resemble those of Eliot Porter, Ansel Adams, or Richard Brown, the important thing to us is that we enjoy them, and our summer hobby allows us to enjoy daylilies throughout the year.

Color and Form

▲ 'Gentle Shepherd'

▲ 'Creative Art'

▲ 'Hope Diamond'

▶ 'Brocaded Gown'

◀ 'Wynnson'

▼ 'Kindly Light' (with *Coreopsis verticillata* 'Moonbeam')

▶ 'Beauty to Behold'

▼ 'Alec Allen'

▲ 'Puddin'

◀ 'Hyperion'

▲ 'Condilla'

▶ 'Betty Woods'

▲ 'Golden Scroll'

▶ 'Dance Ballerina Dance'

▼ 'Janet Gayle' (left)

▼ 'Ruffled Apricot' (right)

 'Siloam Double
Rose'

◀ 'Siloam Double
Classic' (left)

▼ 'Rocket City' (right)

▲ 'Simply Pretty'

▶ 'Pat Mercer'

▲ 'Heather Green'

◄ 'Real Wind'

▶ 'Rose Emily'

▶ 'Seductress'

▲ 'Fairy Tale Pink'

◄ 'Lullaby Baby'

▲ 'Martha Adams'

▲ 'Country Club'

◀ 'Joyful Occasion'

▼ 'Frank Gladney'

▶ 'Barbara Mitchell'

▼ 'New Series'

▲ 'Attribution'

◀ 'Will Return'

▲ 'Sophisticated Miss'

◀ 'Grape Velvet'

◀ 'Elizabeth Anne Hudson' (left)

▼ 'Graceful Eye' (right)

▲ 'Chicago Knobby'

▶ 'Chicago Royal'

▼ 'Russian Rhapsody'

▲ 'Sebastian'

◀ 'Midnight Magic'

▲ 'Douglas Dale'

◀ 'Christmas Is'

▲ 'Pardon Me'

◀ 'Siloam Bo Peep'

▲ 'Siloam Virginia Henson'

▶ 'Siloam Tee Tiny'

CHAPTER 13

Daylily Awards

THE AMERICAN HEMEROCALLIS SOCIETY, through its Awards and Honors Program, presents numerous awards each year to outstanding daylily cultivars in various categories, to members who are honored for outstanding service and/or accomplishment, and for excellent slides and video recordings.

These annual awards and honors, listed in the *Daylily Judges Handbook*, are often named in honor of people who have contributed greatly to further the advancement of *Hemerocallis*. The highest award a cultivar can receive, for example, is the **Stout Silver Medal**, given in memory of Arlow B. Stout, who, as we said earlier, is considered the father of modern daylily breeding in North America. This award can be given only to a plant that has first received the Award of Merit (see below).

The winners are chosen in various ways: by the AHS Board of Directors; by vote of the AHS membership; by special panels of judges; and by the Awards and Honors Judges. Most are presented annually at the Annual Awards and Honors Banquet at the National Convention of the AHS.

Awards presented to outstanding daylilies are of interest to us all, since they show that the plant is outstanding in its field. Some catalogs list with abbreviations the awards received by a cultivar. Wild's catalog, for example, follows the description of Stella de Oro, with: Donn Fischer Memorial Cup, 1979. H.M., 1979. A.M., 1982. S.M., 1985. For definitions of these abbreviations and those of other cultivar awards, see the following list:

A.M. — The Award of Merit is given annually to the ten cultivars that get the most votes by the AHS awards and honors judges from at least one-half of the daylily growing regions. It is given for outstanding beauty and performance over a wide area of the country.

A.T.G. — The Annie T. Giles Award is for the most outstanding small-flowered cultivar with a width measuring 3 to 4H inches.

D.C.S. — The Don C. Stevens Award is given for the best banded or eyed daylily.

D.F. — The Donn Fischer Memorial Cup is for the most outstanding miniature bloom that is less than 3 inches in diameter.

H.M. — Honorable Mention is the first official recognition for excellence beyond the regional level presented to a new cultivar.

I.M. — The Ida Munson Award is given for the best double-flowered daylily.

J.E.M. — The James E. Marsh Award is given for an outstanding purple or lavender cultivar.

J.C. — The Junior Citation is given for new seedlings that have not yet been introduced but show promise.

L.A.A. — The Lenington All-American Award is given for a daylily that has been offered for sale for at least ten years and has performed in an outstanding way in all parts of the country.

L.E.P. — The L. Ernest Plouf Award is given for a consistently fragrant dormant daylily. This includes a monetary award of $500.

R.C.P. — The Richard C. Peck Memorial Award is given for the best tetraploid daylily.

R.P.M. — The Robert P. Miller Medal goes to the best white or near-white tetraploid daylily.

S.M. — The Stout Silver Medal is described above.

Other awards given at the national convention each year include the **President's Cup (P.C.)**, which goes to the most outstanding established clump in a convention tour garden as voted by those attending the meeting. The **Florida Sunshine Cup** is given for a clump with the best small-flowered or miniature blooms in a convention tour garden.

Judging Daylilies

The *Daylily Judge's Handbook* provides detailed instructions for rating daylilies. Hybridizers who wish to enter their plants in competition should certainly order a copy of this manual from the American Hemerocallis Society, and anyone interested in simply understanding "what makes a good daylily" will find detailed definitions listed there (see the Appendix).

AHS judges are of two types: Awards and Honors Judges, who determine the annual awards just mentioned, and Exhibition Judges, who judge at daylily shows and exhibitions. They are well-trained, knowledgeable individuals who attend judging seminars and have strict guidelines to follow. However, as you might expect, these experts do not always agree with each other or with the rest of us, since aesthetic evaluation is an individual perception and beauty cannot always be defined by rules.

The guidelines make the evaluation process as objective as possible, however, by allotting points in various categories with a possible score of 100. The scale of points in the various categories is listed in the *Judge's Handbook* as follows:

1. *Judging Cultivar in Garden.*
   Flower — 45 points
   Scape — 25 points
   Foliage — 10 points
   Complete Plant — 20 points
2. *Judging Cultivar in Exhibition*
   Flower — 50 points
   Scape — 35 points
   Condition and grooming — 15 points

3. *Judging Seedling*
  Flower — 40 points
  Scape — 30 points
  Distinction — 25 points
  Grooming and Condition — 5 points

4. *Judging Single Off-Scape Flower*
  Size, texture, color, size, and condition count 20 points each.

Award Winners to 1990

Stout Silver Medal

1950 Hesperus
1951 Painted Lady
1952 Potentate
1953 Revolute
1954 Dauntless
1955 Prima Donna
1956 Naranja
1957 Ruffled Pinafore
1958 High Noon
1959 Salmon Sheen
1960 Fairy Wings
1961 Playboy
1962 Bess Ross
1963 Multnomah
1964 Frances Fay
1965 Luxury Lace
1966 Cartwheels
1967 Full Reward
1968 Satin Glass
1969 May Hall
1970 Ava Michelle
1971 Renee
1972 Hortensia
1973 Lavender Flight
1974 Winning Ways
1975 Clarence Simon
1976 Green Flutter
1977 Green Glitter
1978 Mary Todd
1979 Moment of Truth
1980 Bertie Mae Ferris
1981 Ed Murray
1982 Ruffled Apricot
1983 Sabie
1984 My Belle
1985 Stella de Oro
1986 Janet Gayle
1987 Becky Lynn
1988 Martha Adams
1989 Brocaded Gown
1990 Fairy Tale Pink

Lenington All-American Awards

1970 Frances Fay and
     Luxury Lace
1971 Satin Glass
1972 Skiatook Cardinal
1973 Green Valley
1974 Winsome Lady
1975 Jest
1976 Clarence Simon
1977 White Formal
1978 Hope Diamond
1979 Oriental Ruby
1980 Green Flutter
1981 Prester John
1982 Raindrop
1983 Ed Murray
1984 Red Rum
1985 Olive Bailey Langdon
1986 Yesterday Memories
1987 Golden Prize
1988 Lullaby Baby
1989 Russian Rhapsody

Donn Fischer Memorial Cup (miniature)

1962 Golden Chimes
1963 Tinker Bell
1964 Curls
1965 Thumbelina
1966 Lula Mae Purnell
1967 Corky
1968 Bitsy
1969 Lona Eaton Miller
1970 Red Mittens
1971 Toyland
1972 Apricot Angel
1973 Bertie Ferris
1974 Squeaky
1975 Little Grapette
1976 Puddin
1977 Butterpat
1978 Raindrop
1979 Stella de Oro
1980 Little Celena
1981 Fox Grape
1982 Siloam June Bug
1983 Siloam Red Toy
1984 Peach Fairy
1985 Pardon Me
1986 Little Zinger
1987 Siloam Tee Tiny
1988 Yellow Lollipop
1989 Siloam Bertie Ferris
1990 Texas Sunlight

Annie T. Giles Award
(small-flowered)

1964 McPick
1965 Luxury Lace
1966 Melon Balls
1967 Little Rainbow
1968 Renee
1969 Little Wart
1970 Green Flutter
1971 Suzie Wong
1972 Guardian Angel
1973 Bambi Doll
1974 Buffys Doll
1975 Little Business
1976 Ed Murray
1977 Little Infant
1978 Little Greenie
1979 Red Rum
1980 Siloam Purple Plum
1981 Lord Camden
1982 Lullaby Baby
1983 Siloam Bo Peep
1984 Wynnson
1985 Siloam Virginia Henson
1986 Chorus Line
1987 Pandora's Box
1988 Siloam Jim Cooper
1989 Sugar Cookie
1990 Janice Brown

James E. Marsh Award
(purple)

1981 Swirling Water
1982 Crown Royal
1983 Sebastian
1984 Siloam Tee Tiny
1985 Royal Heritage
1986 Super Purple
1987 Violet Hour
1988 Hamlet

1989 Graceful Eye
1990 Zinfandel

Robert P. Miller **(white)**

1974 Silver Fan
1975 White Cloud
1976 Olive Langdon
1977 Astolat
1978 Chateau Blanc
1979 Ming Snow
1980 Snowy Apparition
1981 Blanco Real and
     Soft Caress
1982 Gloria Blanca
1983 Snow Ballerina

Ida Munson Award
(double)

1975 Double Cutie
1976 Prester John
1977 Pojo
1978 King Alfred
1979 Peach Souffle
1980 Double Razzle Dazzle
1981 Double Bourbon
1982 Pa Pa Gulino
1983 Betty Woods
1984 Condilla
1985 Yazoo Souffle
1986 Siloam Double Rose
1987 Stroke of Midnight
1988 Siloam Double Classic
1989 Rachael My Love
1990 Cabbage Flower

Harris Olson Award
(spider)

1989 Kindly Light
1990 Lady Fingers

Richard C. Peck Award
(best tetraploid)

1974 Mary Todd
1975 Kings Cloak
1976 Douglas Dale
1977 Ruffled Apricot
1978 Sombrero Way
1979 Chicago Knobby
1980 Dancing Shiva
1981 Apple Tart
1982 Frozen Jade
1983 Midnight Magic

L. Ernest Plouf Award
(fragrance)

1979 Willard Gardner
1980 Tender Love
1981 Frozen Jade
1982 Siloam Double Rose
1983 Ida Miles
1984 Siloam Mama
1985 Siloam Double Classic
1986 Hudson Valley
1987 Evening Bell
1988 Chorus Line
1989 Golden Scroll
1990 Smoky Mountain
     Autumn

Don C. Stephens Award
(eyed or banded)

1985 Siloam Bertie Ferris
1986 Bette Davis Eyes
1987 Paper Butterfly
1988 Will Return
1989 Siloam Virginia Henson
1990 Janice Brown

CHAPTER 14

Favorite Daylilies

A NY LIST of some of the most popular day-lilies currently being grown in North America is certain to enrage hybridizers who wonder why their choice introductions are not mentioned and also may anger gardeners who find that many of their favorites are not listed. To try to pick a few hundred worthy cultivars from more than 32,000 named ones is an impossible task.

In the selection that follows we have chosen some from the "Popularity Poll," the hundred best cultivars chosen by members of the American Hemerocallis Society over the past two decades, and others known to be favorites from our own experience and that of others. Most are available from a wide range of nurseries. The list contains an assortment of evergreens, semi-evergreens, and dormants, and you must use your best judgment when choosing plants that will be suitable for your locality. (See pages 20-22 for information about foliage types and hardiness.)

In addition to the name of the daylily, we also include the hybridizer's name, the date of introduction, approximate blooming time, height of blooming scape, and the size of bloom. (See all of Chapter 3 for a discussion of the special vocabulary used to describe the characteristics of daylilies.) Most descriptions are taken from those in the *Check List* of the American Hemerocallis Society. Note that many of the cultivars not listed as tetraploids have been converted to tets, and in some cases both the diploid and tetraploid forms of the same cultivar are available.

CULTIVAR	COLOR AND FORM
ABSTRACT ART	Bitone of coral amber with honey buff sepals; ruffled
AFTER THE FALL	Tangerine-copper blend with yellow halo and rust eyezone above greenish copper throat
AGAPE LOVE	Pale ivory with pink midribs and green throat
ALAN	Velvety, cherry red with greenish yellow throat
ALEC ALLEN	Creamy yellow with green throat
AMAZING GRACE	Creamy white with pale green throat
AMERICAN BICENTENNIAL	Dusty rose with light chartreuse throat
AMERICAN DREAM	Pale yellow
AMERICAN REVOLUTION	Velvety black-red with green throat
AMY STEWART	Pink with green throat
APPLE TART	Dark red with green throat
ATTRIBUTION	Rose-pink with white midribs and deeper rose eyezone
BAJA	Bright velvety red with green throat
BANDIT MAN	Burnt orange with large, red eyezone and gold throat
BARBARA MITCHELL	An outstanding pink from Fairy Tale Pink
BEAUTY TO BEHOLD	Light lemon with ruffled edges
BECKY LYNN	Rose pink
BEN ARTHUR DAVIS	Yellow-cream with orchid
BENCHMARK	Lavender with cream throat
BERTIE MAE FERRIS	Green-gold with green halo and throat
BEST OF FRIENDS	Deep pink blends with green throat
BETTE DAVIS EYES	Pale lavender with deep purple eyezone
BETTY WOODS	Double yellow with green throat
BITSY	Small, yellow, trumpet-shaped blooms; slightly ruffled petals
BLAKE ALLEN	Large, yellow blooms
BLOSSOM VALLEY	Light orchid-pink, ruffled blooms with gold throat

FOLIAGE TYPE	BLOOM SEASON	SCAPE HEIGHT	BLOSSOM DIAMETER	OTHER CHARACTERISTICS	HYBRIDIZER & DATE
Dormant	M	32"	6"		HALL 1976
Evergreen	EE	20"	2¼"	Fragrant; nocturnal; extended blooms	KIRCHHOFF 1981
Semi-evergreen	M	15"	7"		SPALDING 1976
Dormant	EM	36"	5½"		CLAAR 1953
Evergreen	EM	26"	5½"	Fragrant; extended blooms	CARPENTER 1982
Evergreen	EM	22"	6"		MACMILLAN 1968
Dormant	M	28"	6"	Nocturnal; heavy bloomer	WILD 1980
Semi-evergreen	M	26"	6"	Fragrant	PITTARD 1971
Dormant	M	28"	5½"		WILD 1972
Evergreen	E	26"	6½"		MACMILLAN 1974
Dormant	EM	28"	6"	Nocturnal; tetraploid	HUGHES 1974
Evergreen	EM	24"	7¼"		SPALDING 1976
Semi-evergreen	EM	26"	6"	Tetraploid	DURIO 1974
Dormant	M	28"	5½"	Tetraploid	STEVENS 1979
Semi-evergreen	M	20"	6"		PIERCE 1984
Semi-evergreen	M	26"	5½"	Nocturnal	SELLERS 1978
Semi-evergreen	EE	20"	6½"	Fragrant	GUIDRY 1977
Dormant	M	34"	8"		WILD 1971
Evergreen	M	30"	6"	Fragrant; tetraploid	MUNSON 1980
Dormant	L	26"	5½"	Extended blooms	WINNIFORD 1977
Evergreen	EM	19"	6½"		SPALDING 1975
Evergreen	E	22"	5½"	Fragrant; extended blooms	KIRCHHOFF 1982
Evergreen	E	26"	5½"	Fragrant	KIRCHHOFF 1980
Semi-evergreen	EE	20"	2"	Nocturnal; extended blooms; long blooming season	WARNER 1963
Evergreen	EM	28"	7"	Fragrant; extended blooms	CARPENTER 1981
Dormant	M	18"	6½"	Nocturnal	WILD 1973

EE—extra early   E—early   EM—early midseason   M—midseason   ML—late midseason   L—late
VL—very late   RE—reblooms

CULTIVAR	COLOR AND FORM
BLUE HAPPINESS	Rose-pink with bluish edges
BONNIE JOHN SETON	Pale yellow
BORDER GIANT	Frosty melon pink with orchid rib; rather large bloom for a short scape, but nice anyway
BRIDGET	Black-red with greenish yellow throat
BROCADED GOWN	Lemon yellow with chartreuse throat; ruffled; recurved
BURNING DAYLIGHT	Crimson brushed over bright orange
BUTTERPAT	Yellow
BUTTERSCOTCH RUFFLES	Peach blends with green throat
BUTTER YELLOW	Butter yellow
BY MYSELF	Light orange
CABBAGE FLOWER	Very double, ruffled, lemon yellow flowers
CALL TO REMEMBRANCE	Near white with green throat
CAMDEN GOLD DOLLAR	Golden yellow blooms in round form; ruffled and creped
CAROLYN CRISWELL	Buff yellow
CARTWHEELS	Light orange-gold; heavy producer of large, flat, round blooms
CATHERINE WOODBERY	Light orchid, slightly ruffled blooms
CHALLENGER	Super tall, brick red with a heavy bud count
CHARLES JOHNSON	Cherry red with green throat
CHERRY CHEEKS	Watermelon pink with lavender; small green-yellow throat
CHERRY FESTIVAL	Cherry red with green throat
CHERRY LACE	Cherry rose with creamy pink midrib; very ruffled
CHICAGO FIRE	Red with green throat
CHICAGO KNOBBY	Purple bitone with darker center
CHICAGO QUEEN	Lavender with purple eyezone

FOLIAGE TYPE	BLOOM SEASON	SCAPE HEIGHT	BLOSSOM DIAMETER	OTHER CHARACTERISTICS	HYBRIDIZER & DATE
Semi-evergreen	E	20"	7"	Extended blooms	SPALDING 1975
Dormant	EM	26"	7"	Fragrant; nocturnal; extended blooms	PECK 1967
Dormant	M, RE	16"	7"	Nocturnal	WILD 1973
Semi-evergreen	M	20"	3"		PITTARD 1974
Semi-evergreen	EM	26"	6"	Extended blooms	MILLIKAN 1979
Dormant	M	30"	6"	Extended blooms	FISCHER 1957
Dormant	M	20"	2½"	Fragrant; nocturnal	KENNEDY 1970
Semi-evergreen	E	24"	3"		HARLING 1978
Evergreen	EM	26"	8"		MONETTE 1974
Dormant	M	32"	6½"	Tetraploid	PECK 1971
Semi-evergreen	EE	18"	4½"	Fragrant; extended blooms	KIRCHHOFF 1984
Semi-evergreen	EM	22"	5"		SPALDING 1969
Semi-evergreen	EM	20"	3"		YANCY 1982
Dormant	E	22"	4½"	Extended blooms	HARRIS-PETREE 1977
Dormant	M	30"	7"		LAMBERT 1969
Dormant	ML	30"	6"	Fragrant; extended blooms; wide petals	CHILDS 1967
Evergreen	ML	48"–60"	4½"	Extended blooms; a Stout origination	STOUT 1949
Semi-evergreen	EM	24"	5"	Fragrant; tetraploid	GATES 1981
Dormant	ML	28"	6"	Tetraploid	PECK 1968
Dormant	M	28"	6"		YANCEY-HARRISON 1973
Dormant	M	34"	6"	Nocturnal; extended blooms	WILD 1977
Semi-evergreen	M	34"	6"	Tetraploid	MARSH 1973
Semi-evergreen	EM	22"	6"	Tetraploid	MARSH 1974
Semi-evergreen	EM	28"	6"	Tetraploid	MARSH 1974

EE—extra early   E—early   EM—early midseason   M—midseason   ML—late midseason   L—late VL—very late   RE—reblooms

CULTIVAR	COLOR AND FORM
CHICAGO ROSY	Rosy red; ruffled; heavy bloomer; one of our favorites
CHICAGO ROYAL	Purple bitone with green throat
CHINESE AUTUMN	Coral-orange blend with pale apricot throat
CHINESE SON	Huge, gold blooms distinguish this favorite
CHORUS LINE	Round, ruffled, pink flower with rose band above yellow halo; dark green throat
CHOSEN LOVE	Lavender with green throat
CHRISTMAS IS	Bright red with green throat
CLARENCE SIMON	Pink; ruffled
COLONEL SIMON	Daffodil yellow blooms in large numbers
CONDILLA	Deep gold
COSMIC HUMMINGBIRD	Peach with ruby red eye
COUNTRY CLUB	Baby pink with faint green throat; diamond-dusted
CREATIVE ART	Yellow with green throat
DANCE BALLERINA DANCE	Pink; highly ruffled; widely used as a parent of ruffled cultivars
DANCING SHIVA	Pink blends with greenish throat
DAN TAU	Greenish white with pink hues; green halo
DIAMOND ANNIVERSARY	Velvety; peach-pink blends; rounded blooms
DORETHE LOUISE	Yellow-green with green throat
DOUBLE CUTIE	Chartreuse with green throat
DOUBLE TULIP	Blends of red and yellow
DOUGLAS DALE	Red blend with green throat
ED MURRAY	An outstanding, small-flowering, black-red; a favorite for many years; slightly ruffled petals
EENIE WEENIE	Tiny, yellow blooms with green throat

FOLIAGE TYPE	BLOOM SEASON	SCAPE HEIGHT	BLOSSOM DIAMETER	OTHER CHARACTERISTICS	HYBRIDIZER & DATE
Semi-evergreen	M	25"	6"	Tetraploid	MARSH 1974
Semi-evergreen	M	24"	7"	Tetraploid	MARSH 1970
Evergreen	M	26"	6"	Tetraploid	MUNSON 1973
Dormant	M	32"	7"	Extended blooms; tetraploid	GRIESBACH-CALDWELL 1973
Evergreen	E	20"	3½"	Fragrant; extended blooms	KIRCHHOFF 1981
Semi-evergreen	EM	26"	6"	Fragrant; extended blooms	MAXWELL 1970
Dormant	EM	26"	4½"		YANCEY 1979
Evergreen	M	28"	6"		MACMILLAN 1966
Evergreen	EM	24"	7"	Fragrant	SIMON 1971
Dormant	EM	20"	4½"	Double	GROOMS 1977
Semi-evergreen	EE	26"	3½"	Fragrant; nocturnal; extended blooms	KIRCHHOFF 1977
Dormant	M, RE	18"–20"	6"	Nocturnal	WILD 1974
Semi-evergreen	M	16"	6"		PIERCE 1981
Dormant	M	24"	6"	Tetraploid; all-time favorite	PECK 1976
Dormant	E	22"	5½"	Extended blooms; tetraploid	MOLDOVAN 1974
Semi-evergreen	E	24"	6"		SMITH 1981
Dormant	EM, RE	32"	6½"	Nocturnal; exceptionally vigorous	CHILDS 1966
Dormant	M	18"	6"	Fragrant	PECK 1976
Evergreen	EM	12"	4½"	Double	BROWN 1972
Dormant	M	24"	3"	Extended blooms	MILES 1963
Dormant	M	24"	6"	Tetraploid	PECK 1968
Dormant	M	30"	4"	Extended blooms; fairly sunfast	GROVATT 1970
Dormant	EM	10"	1½"	Extended; one of the first reblooming minatures	ADEN 1976

EE—extra early E—early EM—early midseason M—midseason ML—late midseason L—late VL—very late RE—reblooms

CULTIVAR	COLOR AND FORM
ELFIN	Orange; blooms are often buried in a mass of taller-growing foliage
ELIZABETH ANNE HUDSON	Peach-rose, edged purple with darker eyezone
ELIZABETH YANCEY	Light pink with a green throat
ELSIE SPALDING	Ivory blushed with pink; pale pink halo
EMERALD DEW	Yellow with green throat
ERIN PRAIRIE	Green-gold with bright green throat
EVENING BELL	Yellow with greenish yellow throat
FABULOUS FAVORITE	Raspberry red with chartreuse throat
FABULOUS PRIZE	Pink with green throat
FAIRY TALE PINK	Shell pink; ruffled edges with darker veining
FLORENCE BYRD	Light yellow with green throat
FRANK GLADNEY	Coral pink; rounded form; gold throat
FRANS HALS	Bicolor: rusty red petals and orange sepals
FROZEN JADE	Lemon yellow; slightly ruffled and recurved
GENTLE SHEPHERD	One of the whitest near-whites; flat, ruffled blooms; small, green throat
GEORGE CUNNINGHAM	Ruffled melon with faint lavender midrib; green-gold throat
GLORIA BLANCA	Near-white; green throat
GOLDEN PRIZE	Ruffled gold
GOLDEN SCROLL	Ruffled blooms of blends of tangerine and gold; diamond-dusted, recurved blooms
GRACEFUL EYE	Lavender with purple halo and green throat
GRAND CANYON	Lavender bicolor

FOLIAGE TYPE	BLOOM SEASON	SCAPE HEIGHT	BLOSSOM DIAMETER	OTHER CHARACTERISTICS	HYBRIDIZER & DATE
Dormant	EE	2"–8"	3"	Extended blooms; a novelty, valued for extra earliness; one of the shortest scapes	STOUT 1949
Evergreen	EM	26"	5½"	Tetraploid	MUNSON 1975
Evergreen	E	28"	5½"	Extended blooms	YANCEY-HARRISON 1973
Evergreen	M	14"	6"	Extended blooms	SPALDING 1985
Dormant	EM	28"	6½"	Extended blooms; tetraploid	HARRIS 1980
Dormant	EM	27"	6½"		FAY 1971
Dormant	EM	22"	7"	Nocturnal; extended blooms; tetraploid	PECK 1971
Semi-evergreen	EM	26"	7"		LANKART 1968
Evergreen	E	27"	5"	Extended blooms	BROWN 1974
Semi-evergreen	M	24"	5½"		PIERCE 1980
Evergreen	EM	24"	6"	Tetraploid	PECK 1970
Evergreen	EM	26"	6½"	Tetraploid	DURIO 1979
Dormant	ML	24"	5"		FLORY 1955
Dormant	M	28"	5½"	Fragrant; nocturnal; tetraploid	SELLERS 1975
Semi-evergreen	EM	28"	5½"		YANCY 1980
Dormant	ML	36"	5½"	Extended blooms; heavy bloomer	HALL 1957
Dormant	M	22"	6"	Extended blooms; tetraploid	HARRIS 1979
Dormant	L	26"	7"	Tetraploid; heavy bud count	PECK 1968
Dormant	E	20"	5½"	Fragrant	GUIDRY 1983
Evergreen	E	21"	6"		SPALDING 1981
Evergreen	EM	32"	6"–7"	Extended blooms	FARRIS 1957

EE—extra early   E—early   EM—early midseason   M—midseason   ML—late midseason   L—late
VL—very late   RE—reblooms

CULTIVAR	COLOR AND FORM
GRANDFATHER TIME	Brick red with gold throat; huge blooms
GRAND OPERA	Rose-red with green throat
GRAND WAYS	Lavender-rose; diamond-dusted; ruffled; giant blooms
GRAPE VELVET	Concord grape–purple; ruffled
GREEN FLUTTER	Rich canary yellow; slightly ruffled with green throat
GREEN GLITTER	Light yellow with chartreuse throat; ruffled; diamond dusted; heavy bud count
GREEN ICE	Pale yellow with green throat
GREEN PUFF	Canary yellow, round, full blooms with green throats
GREEN SPIDER	Greenish yellow; true spider
GUARDIAN ANGEL	Near-white with light green throat
GUSTO	Extremely vigorous plants produce red blooms in large numbers
HARRY BARRAS	Cream yellow
HAUNTING MELODY	Strong fuchsia-rose color; heavily ruffled
HAZEL MONETTE	Pink with green throat
HEATHER GREEN	Apple-blossom pink with edge of gold on petals that are lightly ruffled
HIGHLAND LORD	Deep red-wine with lemon throat
HOME RUN	Bright orange; huge, rather flat blooms
HOMEWARD BOUND	Light peach with pink overcast
HOPE DIAMOND	A superior near-white
HUDSON VALLEY	Light yellow with green throat; huge blooms
HYPERION	Bright lemon yellow
ICE CARNIVAL	Near-white, diamond-dusted, wide-petaled blooms with yellow-green throat; petals are almost translucent
IRON GATE ICEBERG	Near-white with green throat

FOLIAGE TYPE	BLOOM SEASON	SCAPE HEIGHT	BLOSSOM DIAMETER	OTHER CHARACTERISTICS	HYBRIDIZER & DATE
Dormant	EM	30"	7½"		WILD 1966
Semi-evergreen	EM	26"	6"	Tetraploid	MUNSON 1978
Dormant	EM	26"	7"		WILD 1976
Dormant	M	24"	5"		WILD 1978
Semi-evergreen	ML	22"	3½"	Extended blooms	WILLIAMSON 1964
Semi-evergreen	EM	32"	6"–7"	Blooms last well into evening	HARRISON 1964
Semi-evergreen	ML	36"	7"	Good fragrance; nocturnal; extended blooms	SCHREINER 1963
Semi-evergreen	M	15"	5½"	Extended blooms	SPALDING 1977
Dormant	EM	32"		Fragrant; extended blooms	TERRY 1970
Semi-evergreen	EM	26"	4"		GORE-MURPHY 1964
Dormant	EM	24"	5"	Value increased by earliness	HALL 1955
Evergreen	EM	26"	7"		MONETTE 1974
Dormant	EM, RE	36"	6"	Vigorous; heavy bloomer	WILD 1974
Evergreen	EM	22"	6"		MONETTE 1973
Dormant	EM	30"	5"	Tetraploid	PECK 1968
Semi-evergreen	ML	22"	5"	Tetraploid; double	MUNSON 1983
Dormant	EM	30"	6½"		WILD 1967
Evergreen	ML	16"	8"	Extended blooms	SPALDING 1976
Dormant	EM	14"	4"		MACMILLAN 1968
Dormant	M	32"	8"	Tetraploid; blooms open at night and last all next day	PECK 1971
Dormant	M	40"	5½"	Fragrant; extended blooms (several weeks); blooms well into evening; blooms heavily	MEAD 1924
Dormant	M	28"	6"	Fragrant; extended blooms	CHILDS 1967
Evergreen	M	26"	6"	Fragrant; nocturnal	SELLERS 1972

EE—extra early   E—early   EM—early midseason   M—midseason   ML—late midseason   L—late VL—very late   RE—reblooms

CULTIVAR	COLOR AND FORM
JANET GAYLE	Creamy pink with green throat; heavy substance
JEAN WOOTEN	Golden yellow; ruffled; diamond-dusted with heavy bud count
JENNY SUE	Huge, ruffled, pale peach blooms; diamond-dusted
JEROME	Orange with darker eyezone; green throat
JIMS PICK	Pink blends that change throughout the day
JOAN SENIOR	Near-white with flat or slightly recurved blooms; ruffled; heavy bud count
JOCK RANDALL	Reddish pink with green throat
JOEL	Yellow with green throat
JOEY LANGDON	Bright velvety red with green throat; heavy bud count
JOYFUL OCCASION	Deep pink with green throat
KATE CARPENTER	Creamy melon pink with cream throat; round, flat blooms
KECIA	Rose-pink
KINDLY LIGHT	Classic yellow spider of huge size
KINGS CLOAK	Wine-rose blend with mauve-wine eyezone; green-yellow throat
LAKE NORMAN SUNSET	Blend of pinks with white midrib
LEMOINE BECHTOLD	Rose blends of unusual beauty; ruffled
LITTLE BRANDY	Pink blends on short plant
LITTLE BUSINESS	Rose-red with bluish cast
LITTLE DEEKE	Orange-gold blends with green throat; creped petals
LITTLE GRAPETTE	Grape purple
LITTLE GREENIE	Yellow-green with green throat
LITTLE INFANT	Near-white with green throat
LITTLE RAINBOW	Pink, cream, orchid, and yellow blends; orange throat
LITTLE WOMEN	Buff pink with cherry red eyezone
LITTLE ZINGER	Red with deep green throat

FOLIAGE TYPE	BLOOM SEASON	SCAPE HEIGHT	BLOSSOM DIAMETER	OTHER CHARACTERISTICS	HYBRIDIZER & DATE
Evergreen	E	26"	6½"	Fragrant	GUIDRY 1976
Evergreen	EM	28"	5"	Fragrant; extended blooms	KIRCHHOFF 1976
Dormant	ML, RE	24"	8"		HALL 1967
Evergreen	EM	22"	6½"	Extended blooms	SPALDING 1979
Dormant	EM	38"	7"	Best in full sun	WILD 1973
Evergreen	EM	24"	6"	Extended blooms	DURIO 1977
Dormant	M	28"	6"	Extended blooms; tetraploid	PECK 1970
Dormant	EM	24"	5½"	Extended blooms; tetraploid	HARRIS 1978
Dormant	M	32"	5"	Tetraploid	GRIESBACH-HARDY 1970
Evergreen	M	20"	6"	Extended blooms	SPALDING 1976
Evergreen	EM	28"	6"	Fragrant; tetraploid	MUNSON 1980
Evergreen	M	26"	6"	Extended blooms	MUNSON 1966
Dormant	M	28"	8"	Extended blooms	BECHTOLD 1950
Evergreen	EM	24"	6"	Extended blooms; tetraploid	MUNSON 1969
Semi-evergreen	EM	18"	6"	Fragrant; extended blooms	CARPENTER 1979
Dormant	M	30"	7"		WILD 1967
Evergreen	EE	20"	5"	Fragrant; nocturnal; extended blooms	GUIDRY 1979
Semi-evergreen	EM	15"	3"	Extended blooms	MAXWELL 1971
Evergreen	EE	20"	4"	Fragrant	GUIDRY 1980
Semi-evergreen	E	12"	2"	Extended blooms	WILLIAMSON 1970
Evergreen	M	18"	4"		WINNIFORD 1972
Evergreen	M	20"	4"		MONETTE 1973
Dormant	EM	24"	2"		RECKAMP 1963
Dormant	EM	26"	2½"		WILD 1971
Semi-evergreen	EM	16"	2½"		LANKART 1979

EE—extra early   E—early   EM—early midseason   M—midseason   ML—late midseason   L—late VL—very late   RE—reblooms

CULTIVAR	COLOR AND FORM
LORD CAMDEN	Bright crimson-raspberry
LOUISE LATHAM	Golden yellow with green throat
LOVELY DANCER	Pale peach-amber overlaid with rose; diamond-dusted and ruffled
LULLABY BABY	Creamy pink; lightly ruffled
LUSTY LEALAND	Apricot melon with green-yellow throat
LUXURY LACE	Light lavender with yellow throat
MABEL NOLEN	Red-rose with green throat; ruffled
MAE GRAHAM	Pink blends
MARTHA ADAMS	Pink with green throat
MARY TODD	Buff yellow with lighter midribs; heavy bud count and vigorous
MASTER TOUCH	Ruffled pink with tangerine throat
MAUNA LOA	Gold blends with an edge of dark red
MAVIS SMITH	Creamy pink, flat blooms; heavy bud count
MELODY LANE	Creamy pink with darker blends; chartreuse throat; heavy bud count
MELON BALLS	Melon with orchid overtones; gold throat
MIDNIGHT MAGIC	Black-red with green throat; vigorous
MILK CHOCOLATE	One of the few brown daylilies
MONICA MARIE	Near-white with green throat
MOST NOBLE	Yellow
MOUNTAIN VIOLET	Violet-purple with darker band; green throat
MUMBO JUMBO	Rose-pink bitone with darker halo; green throat
MY BELLE	Flesh pink with green throat
MY CHILDREN	Lavender-pink with green throat
MY PEGGY	Creamy blend with green throat
MYSTERY VALLEY	Coral-pink, ruffled blooms with greenish gold heart

FOLIAGE TYPE	BLOOM SEASON	SCAPE HEIGHT	BLOSSOM DIAMETER	OTHER CHARACTERISTICS	HYBRIDIZER & DATE
Dormant	M	24"	4"		KENNEDY 1974
Semi-evergreen	E	20"	4"		GUIDRY-MACMILLAN 1977
Dormant	M, RE	24"	6½"		HALL 1971
Semi-evergreen	EM	14"	3½"	Fragrant; extended blooms	SPALDING 1975
Dormant	M	28"	6"	Extended blooms; tetraploid	PECK 1970
Dormant	M	32"	4"	Fragrant	SPALDING 1959
Dormant	EM	28"	6"		NOLEN 1984
Evergreen	M	18"	6½"	Extended blooms	SPALDING 1977
Evergreen	EM	19"	6½"	Extended blooms	SPALDING 1979
Semi-evergreen	EM	26"	6"	Tetraploid	FAY 1967
Dormant	EM	30"	6"		HALL 1964
Dormant	EM	22"	5"	Tetraploid	ROBERTS 1976
Semi-evergreen	M	33"	5"	Extended blooms	LENINGTON 1974
Dormant	M	34"	5"	Extended blooms	HALL 1955
Dormant	M	32"	3½"		WILD 1960
Evergreen	EM	28"	5½"	Extended blooms; tetraploid	KINNEBREW 1979
Dormant	M	26"	5"		CARNEY 1967
Evergreen	EM	24"	5"	Fragrant; tetraploid	GATES 1982
Evergreen	M	28"	6"	Fragrant; tetraploid	MUNSON 1980
Evergreen	M	28"	5"	Tetraploid	MUNSON 1973
Semi-evergreen	E	21"	6"	Fragrant; nocturnal; extended blooms	GUIDRY 1979
Evergreen	E	26"	6½"	Extended blooms	DURIO 1973
Evergreen	EM	20"	6"		MONETTE 1975
Semi-evergreen	E	29"	7"		MACMILLAN 1972
Dormant	ML, RE	28"	5"–6"		HALL 1972

EE—extra early   **E**—early   **EM**—early midseason   **M**—midseason   **ML**—late midseason   **L**—late
VL—very late   **RE**—reblooms

CULTIVAR	COLOR AND FORM
New England Night	Black-red
New Series	Clear pink with red eyezone
Neyron Rose	Deep rose-pink with white midribs
Oallie Double	Light yellow, fully double blooms
Oallie Summer	Rich red with darker eyezone; outstanding bud builder
Olive Bailey Langdon	Purple with yellow-green throat
Olivier Monette	Purple with yellow-green throat; widely used in attempts to produce a blue daylily
Ono	Pale yellow with green throat
Oriental Ruby	Carmine red with green throat
Pandora's Box	Creamy white with purple eyezone
Pa Pa Gulino	Silvery flesh pink with rose over green throat
Paper Butterfly	Creamy peach with blue-violet blends; blue-violet eyezone
Pardon Me	Dark wine-red with yellow-green throat; heavy bud count
Pass Me Not	Creamy yellow with maroon-red eyezone
Pat Mercer	Orange with lighter halo and green throat
Paul Bunyan	Light gold, diamond-dusted, huge, ruffled blooms
Pink Limeade	Pink-yellow blends with lime throat
Pojo	Dark yellow; double
Pony Ride	Light golden yellow with green throat
Poogie	Pink with green-yellow throat
Prairie Blue Eyes	Lavender with wide bluish halo; heavy bloomer
Prairie Charmer	Melon pink with dark purple-blue eyezone; green throat
Prairie Moonlight	Huge creamy yellow with piecrust edging
Precious One	Creamy pale pink; brighter pink midribs; diamond-dusted
Prester John	Orange, fully double blooms
Puddin	Flat, full, yellow blooms with green throat

FOLIAGE TYPE	BLOOM SEASON	SCAPE HEIGHT	BLOSSOM DIAMETER	OTHER CHARACTERISTICS	HYBRIDIZER & DATE
Dormant	M	24"	5"	Tetraploid	STEVENS 1978
Semi-evergreen	M	25"	7½"	Extended blooms	CARPENTER 1982
Dormant	M	36"	5"		KRAUS 1950
Dormant	M	20"	5"	Tetraploid	DARROW 1974
Dormant	EM–VL	36"	6"		DARROW 1974
Semi-evergreen	EM	28"	5"	Tetraploid	MUNSON 1974
Evergreen	EM	22"	6"		MONETTE 1973
Evergreen	EM	18"	4"	Fragrant; extended blooms	JOHNSON 1977
Dormant	ML	34"	6"		FISCHER 1968
Evergreen	EM	18"	4"	Fragrant	TALBOTT 1980
Semi-evergreen	E	26"	6"	Extended blooms; tetraploid	DURIO 1977
Semi-evergreen	E	24"	6"	Tetraploid	MORSS 1983
Dormant	M	18"	2½"		APPS 1982
Semi-evergreen	EM	24"	5½"		MACMILLAN-KENNON 1970
Semi-evergreen	M	28"	7"	Nocturnal	JOINER 1982
Dormant	M, RE	40"	8"–9"	Nocturnal	WILD 1978
Dormant	EM	29"	6"		WILD 1972
Semi-evergreen	E	20"	3"		WINNIFORD 1972
Evergreen	M	16"	4½"		SPALDING 1974
Dormant	M	19"	5"	Tetraploid	PECK 1978
Semi-evergreen	M	28"	5½"		MARSH 1970
Dormant	EM	20"	5½"		MARSH 1962
Semi-evergreen	M	34"	8"	Stays open late at night	MARSH 1965
Dormant	EM	20"	6"		HALL 1967
Dormant	EM	26"	5"	Fragrant	ALLGOOD 1971
Dormant	M	20"	2½"	Nocturnal	KENNEDY 1972

EE—extra early   E—early   EM—early midseason   M—midseason   ML—late midseason   L—late   VL—very late   RE—reblooms

CULTIVAR	COLOR AND FORM
PUMPKIN PUDDING	Orange with pink; raised midrib; dark gold throat
QUINN BUCK	Lavender with green throat
RACHAEL MY LOVE	Golden yellow; double
RADIANT GREETINGS	Orange-yellow; wide, dark red halo; ruffled petals
RAINDROP	Light yellow; vigorous
REAL WIND	Pink with wide, light orange halo; small ruffles
RED RUM	Red with touch of lavender; faint halo
ROCKET CITY	Orange with deeper halo of burnt orange
RONDA	Flesh pink with lavender midribs; green throat
ROSE EMILY	Round, rose, recurved petals; green throat
ROSE SWAN	Bright rose with green throat
ROSELLA SHERIDAN	Pink with green throat
ROSETTE	Rich pink with green throat
RUBRIC	Bright red with darker eyezone
RUFFLED APRICOT	Deep apricot with lavender pink midribs; ruffled
RUFFLED IVORY	Near-white with chartreuse-green throat
RUSSIAN RHAPSODY	Triangular-shaped blossoms of plum-purple; yellow-green throat; dark purple eye
SABIE	Golden yellow; ruffled edge
SADIE LOU	Creamy pink with green throat
SARI	Blend of rose, orchid, and pink tints; heavy texture
SCARLOCK	Red with green throat
SEBASTIAN	Purple with lime-green throat
SEDUCTOR	Bright red with green throat

FOLIAGE TYPE	BLOOM SEASON	SCAPE HEIGHT	BLOSSOM DIAMETER	OTHER CHARACTERISTICS	HYBRIDIZER & DATE
Dormant	ML	28"	6"	Tetraploid	WILD 1981
Dormant	M	26"	7"	Tetraploid	PECK 1976
Evergreen	EM	18"	5"	Fragrant; extended blooms	TALBOTT 1983
Dormant	M	38"	5½"	Nocturnal	WILD 1975
Semi-evergreen	M	12"	2"	Fragrant; extended blooms	KENNEDY 1972
Dormant	ML	26"	6"	Tetraploid; tends to rebloom	WILD 1977
Semi-evergreen	M	18"	4"	Extended blooms	PITTARD 1974
Dormant	EM	36"	7"	Tetraploid; impressive in a clump	HARDY 1967
Semi-evergreen	M	26"	6½"		SIKES 1981
Semi-evergreen	M	18"	5"		PIERCE 1982
Evergreen	M	22"	6½"	Extended blooms	SPALDING 1978
Evergreen	M	21"	6½"	Extended blooms	SPALDING 1976
Semi-evergreen	M	20"	6"		SPALDING 1974
Dormant	M	24"	5½"	Tetraploid	GRIESBACH-CALDWELL 1973
Dormant	EM	28"	7"	Fragrant; extended blooms; tetraploid	BAKER 1972
Semi-evergreen	M	27"	5½"		BROWN 1982
Semi-evergreen	M	32"	5½"	Tetraploid	MUNSON 1973
Evergreen	E	24"	6"		MACMILLIAN 1974
Evergreen	M	19"	5½"		SPALDING 1978
Semi-evergreen	M	26"	6"		MUNSON 1983
Dormant	EM	30"	6½"	Tetraploid	PECK 1974
Evergreen	EM	20"	5½"		WILLIAMS 1978
Evergreen	EE	18"	6"	Fragrant; extended blooms; tetraploid	GATES 1983

EE—extra early   E—early   EM—early midseason   M—midseason   ML—late midseason   L—late   VL—very late   RE—reblooms

CULTIVAR	COLOR AND FORM
SEDUCTRESS	Beige-lavender bitone with purple halo; deep green throat; ruffled purple border
SENT FROM HEAVEN	Light pink with green throat
SHIBUI SPLENDOR	Pink with chartreuse throat
SHOCKWAVE	Creamy, golden yellow with green throat
SILOAM BO PEEP	Orchid-pink with dark purple eyezone; green throat
SILOAM BUTTON BOX	Creamy white with maroon eyezone; green throat
SILOAM DOUBLE CLASSIC	Bright pink with green throat
SILOAM DOUBLE ROSE	Pale rose-pink with ruby eyezone
SILOAM TEE TINY	Orchid with purple eyezone
SILOAM VIRGINIA HENSON	Round, pink flower with ruby-red eyezone; green throat
SILVER CIRCUS	Bright yellow, huge, ruffled, blooms with pink infusion; green throat
SIMPLY PRETTY	Deep persimmon with green throat
SKI CHALET	Light yellow with green throat
SO LOVELY	Near-white with green throat
SOMBRERO WAY	Apricot-orange blends with a darker throat
SOPHISTICATED MISS	Pink with rose halo; green throat
SOUND AND FURY	Bright orange-red with green-gold throat
STELLA DE ORO	This canary yellow miniature has stayed on the popularity lists for years because of its long blooming season; it has also been used extensively for breeding other long bloomers
SUGAR CANDY	Bluish orchid with apricot throat
SUGAR COOKIE	Creamy white with green throat
SUN KING	Golden yellow with gold throat
SUPER DOUBLE DELIGHT	Yellow with green throat
SUPER PURPLE	Deep purple with lime-green throat

FOLIAGE TYPE	BLOOM SEASON	SCAPE HEIGHT	BLOSSOM DIAMETER	OTHER CHARACTERISTICS	HYBRIDIZER & DATE
Evergreen	EM	18"	5½"	Fragrant; tetraploid	GATES 1979
Evergreen	EM	18"	6"	Extended blooms	SPALDING 1976
Evergreen	EM	20"	6"	Fragrant	MUNSON 1974
Semi-evergreen	E	32"	6"		BROWN 1978
Dormant	EM	20"	4½"	Fragrant; extended blooms	HENRY 1978
Dormant	EM	20"	4½"		HENRY 1976
Dormant	EM	16"	5"	Double; fragrant; extended blooms	HENRY 1985
Dormant	M	20"	5"	Double; fragrant; extended blooms	HENRY 1979
Dormant	M	20"	3½"		HENRY 1981
Evergreen	EM	18"	4"	Extended blooms	HENRY 1979
Dormant	EM	30"	7"	Fragrant; nocturnal	WILD 1978
Dormant	M	32"	6"	Tetraploid	SELLERS 1978
Semi-evergreen	EM	18"	6"	Extended blooms	KIRK 1972
Semi-evergreen	M	30"	5½"		LENINGTON 1969
Dormant	ML	24"	5½"	Tetraploid	RECKAMP 1973
Semi-evergreen	E	21"	6½"		SPALDING 1973
Semi-evergreen	M	26"	5½"	Tetraploid	SIKES 1978
Dormant	E–L	12"–18"	2½"	Extended blooms	JABLONSKI 1975
Dormant	M	34"	5"		WILD 1973
Evergreen	EM	21"	3½"	Fragrant	APPS 1983
Evergreen	EM	30"	6"	Fragrant; tetraploid	MUNSON 1980
Evergreen	M	30"	7½"	Double; fragrant; extended blooms	MCFARLAND 1978
Semi-evergreen	M	26"	5½"	Fragrant; extended blooms	DOVE 1979

EE—extra early   E—early   EM—early midseason   M—midseason   ML—late midseason   L—late
VL—very late   RE—reblooms

CULTIVAR	COLOR AND FORM
SUSAN ELIZABETH	Huge, light yellow polychrome with small, green throat
TENDER LOVE	Flesh pink; low-growing; late-blooming
TIJUANA	Rosy red, velvety blooms; green-yellow throat
TINY PUMPKIN	Bright orange with green throat
TOO MARVELOUS	Melon-pink blends with green throat
TOP HONORS	Huge, pale yellow blooms, with green throat; creped; diamond-dusted
VIOLA PARKER	Rose-pink with large, yellow throat
VIRACOCHA	Tangerine with yellow throat; lavender midribs; heavy bud count
WASHINGTONS FAREWELL	Lavender-rose with large, yellow throat
WHEN I DREAM	Velvety; blood red with wide, lemon-green throat; heavy bud count
WHITE FORMAL	Near-white with green throat
WILL RETURN	Peach-pink; purple halo; green throat
WIND SONG	Creamy bloom with pink blush; creamy white throat
WINNING WAYS	Greenish yellow with small, green throat
WINSOME LADY	Pale bluish pink with green throat
WITCHES DANCE	Clear, dark red with green throat
WYNN	Yellow with green throat
WYNNSON	Pale yellow with green throat
YASMIN	Blend of creamy yellow and pink
YAZOO SOUFFLE	Light apricot pink
YESTERDAY MEMORIES	Deep pink with green throat
ZAIDEE WILLIAMS	Creamy pink blends with green throat

FOLIAGE TYPE	BLOOM SEASON	SCAPE HEIGHT	BLOSSOM DIAMETER	OTHER CHARACTERISTICS	HYBRIDIZER & DATE
Dormant	EM	28"	7½"	Fragrant; extended blooms; tetraploid	BARTH 1982
Dormant	L	22"	6½"	Extended blooms	YANCEY-HARRISON 1970
Dormant	M	36"	6½"		WILD 1967
Evergreen	EM	20"	2½"		HUDSON 1975
Dormant	M	24"	5"		SELLERS 1975
Semi-evergreen	M	24"	7½"	Fragrant; extended blooms	CHILDS 1976
Evergreen	E	32"	6"		MACMILLAN 1966
Semi-evergreen	EM	25"	7"	Fragrant; tetraploid	ROBERTS 1975
Dormant	EM	30"	7½"		WILD 1972
Semi-evergreen	M	28"	6"		YANCEY 1979
Semi-evergreen	M	30"	5½"	Extended blooms	LENINGTON 1965
Evergreen	M	18"	4½"	Extended blooms	SPALDING 1983
Semi-evergreen	M	28"	6"	Fragrant; extended blooms	BRYANT 1974
Dormant	EM	32"	6"		WILD 1963
Dormant	EM	24"	5½"	Fragrant	GATES 1964
Dormant	EM	30"	6½"	Nocturnal; tetraploid	PECK 1976
Dormant	M	28"	4½"	Extended blooms	CRISWELL 1975
Dormant	EM	24"	4½"	Extended blooms	CRISWELL 1975
Semi-evergreen	EM	30"	6"	Fragrant; tetraploid	MUNSON 1969
Semi-evergreen	EM	26"	6"	Extended blooms	SMITH 1983
Evergreen	M	19"	6½"	Fragrant; extended blooms	SPALDING 1976
Evergreen	EM	23"	5½"		MACMILLAN 1973

EE—extra early   E—early   EM—early midseason   M—midseason   ML—late midseason   L—late   VL—very late   RE—reblooms

CHAPTER 15

Useful Lists of Daylilies

WHEN YOU ARE SEARCHING for a daylily of a particular sort, you may want to consult catalogs with the following lists in hand. The cultivars listed are, of course, only a few of those available in each category. They include:

Extra-Early Bloomers (below)

Early Bloomers (below)

Late Bloomers (page 185)

Bloom over a Long Period (page 185)

Browns (page 186)

Purples (page 186)

Near-Whites (page 186)

Blotches and Halos (page 186)

Fragrant (page 186)

Outstanding Doubles (page 186)

Good Late Doubles (page 186)

Outstanding Ruffles (page 186)

Double Miniatures (page 187)

Miniatures (page 187)

Giant Blooms (page 187)

Spiders and Near-Spiders (page 187)

Extra-Early Bloomers

Bitsy
Butterscotch Ruffles
Citation
Cosmic
Hummingbird
Dee Dee
Dumortieri
Enchanted Elf
Flavina
Gem

Lemon Daylily
Lilac Greetings
Little Bronzene
May Splash
Pony Ride
Sooner Gold
Stella de Oro
Susie Wong
Thumbelina

Early Bloomers

Admiral
American
  Revolution
Believe It
Bell Tel
Bitsy
Burlesque
Call to
  Remembrance
Charming Heart

Child Bride
Copper Rose
Diamond
  Anniversary
Double Pompom
Fairy Delight
Firecup
Flag Day
Florence Byrd
Grand Ways

Early Bloomers continued

Grape Harvest
Gusto
Hyperion
Lemoine Bechtold
Little Women
Magic Age
Neyron Rose
Orangeman
Outrageous
Passing By
Persian Princess
Pink Snow Flakes
Rajah

Sandalwood
Shola
Siloam Space Age
Sleigh Ride
Sooner Gold
Spring Fantasy
Stella de Oro
Step This Way
Sweet Success
Talisman
Tangerine
Tinker Bell
Windchimes

Bloom Over a Long Period

Angel Unawares
Becky Lynn
Bitsy
Buttered Popcorn
Butterscotch Ruffles
Carolina Cranberry
Camden Gold Dollar
Chicago Knobby
Dancing Shiva
Dan Tau
Demetrius
Dr. Kraus
Embassy
Father Time
French Porcelain
Grand Ways
Jakarta
Jersey Spider
Joyful Occasion

Lake Norman Sunset
Lemon Lollipop
Little Deeke
Little Purple Eyes
Louise Manelis
Lullaby Lady
Marie Babin
Mint Tint
My Belle
Olive Bailey Langdon
Oriental Ruby
Pixie Parasol
Queen's Grace
Royal Ambassador
Smarty Pants
So Lovely
Star Dreams
Stella de Oro
Will Return

Late Bloomers

Abstract Art
Alice
Angel
Apple Tart
August Flame
Autumn Daffodil
Autumn Queen
Bee Haven
Blaze of Fire
Border Giant
Breakaway
Bright Banner
Bronze Knight
Chicago Rosy
Cream Desire
Crystal Rose
Cup of Sugar
Disneyland
Double Gold
Double Peach
Double Tulip
Downing Street
Fabulous Flame
Fairy Delight
Formal Affair
Frans Hals
Full Reward
George Cunningham
Good Fortune
Graham Bell
Green Flutter
Hallowell
Helamam
Holiday Delight
Hot Toddy
Intricate Art
Jenny Sue
Kinfolk
Lily Dache
Lovely Dancer

Lydia Bechtold
Million Choir
Modern Classic
Mystery Valley
Mystic Lady
Oallie August Red
Oallie Autumn Gold
Oallie Late Show
Party Partner
Paul Bunyan
Peppermint Parfait
Pink Charm
Pink Swan
Prairie Charmer
Precious One
Princess Irene
Rose Hall
Rose Moss
Rosy Image
Rubens
Rubric
Silent World
Siloam Love
Smoky Joe
So Lovely
Sombrero Way
Spring Chimes
Street Fair
Sunset Echoes
Tahitian Isle
Talisman
Tijuana
Washingtons
    Farewell
Wickerwork
Wild Era
Wild Fancy
Wild Lemonade
Windsor Castle

Browns

Belle Amber
Milk Chocolate

Purples

Blue Lustre
Chicago Royal Purple
Chicago
Weathermaster
Clover Dale
Grape Harvest
Grape Velvet
Jockey Club
Purple Quest
Royal Blueblood
Royal Flair
Russian Rhapsody
Tiffany Jeane

Near-Whites

Beauty Forecast
Blessed Trinity
Call to Remembrance
Chicago Dawn
Fragrant Snow
Guardian Angel
Hope Diamond
Ice Carnival
Iron Gate Iceberg
Jenny Sue
Joan Senior
Ski Chalet
Sugar Cookie
White Fantasy
White Formal
White Temptation
Young Countess

Blotches or Halos

Bandit Man
Better Believe It
Bette Davis Eyes
Chicago Maid
Clincher
Coming Out Party
Dune Dark Eyes
Frame Up
Gallant Eyes
Guardian Angel
Heady Wine
Holiday Delight
Outrageous
Paper Butterfly
Radiant Greetings
Raging Tiger
Rocket City
Sea Warrior
Shady Lady
Siloam Bertie Ferris
Siloam Button Box
Smoke Rings
Varsity

Fragrant

Emerald Sachet
Evening Bell
Fairy Charm
Fragrant Light
Frozen Jade
Glen Ryan
Grand Duchess
Harvest Green
Hudson Valley
Hyperion
Ida Miles
Lemon Daylily
Oriental Princess
Patrice
Siloam Mama
So Lovely
So Sweet
Star Princess
Tender Love
Top Honors

Outstanding Ruffles

Call Girl
Cee Tee
Dance Ballerina
  Dance
Decatur Rhythm
Earth Angel
Ever So Ruffled
Fairy Tale Pink
Martha Adams
Pearl Lewis
Pink Ballerina
Saffron Glow
Strawberry Rose

Outstanding Doubles

Beds of Clouds
Betty Woods
Bobby Gerald
Brent Gabriel
Condilla
Double Bourbon
Double Cutie
Double Dream
Double Firecracker
Double Gold
Double Grapette
Double Old Ivory
Double Peach
Double Razzle Dazzle
Excitable
Forbidden City
Melody Fair
Mother Superior
Pa Pa Gulino
Pojo
Prester John
Siloam Double Rose
Siloam Pure Gold
Stroke of Midnight
Yazoo Powder Puff
Yazoo Souffle

Good Late Doubles

Double Butterscotch
Double Classic
Beauty
Double Decker
Double Talk
Super Double Delight
Twin Dragons

Miniatures

(Low-growing with Small Blooms)

After the Fall
Apricot Angel
Bertie Mae Ferris
Bitsy
Butterpat
Childrens Festival
Corky
Curls
Decatur Imp
Elf Caps
Elfin Imp
Golden Chimes
Little Celena
Little Delight
Little Fantastic
Little Grapette
Little Men
Little Much
Little Rainbow
Little Show Off
Littlest Angel
Little Women
Little Zinger
Lona Eaton Miller
Lula Mae Purnell
Melon Balls
Miniature King
Mini Stella
Pardon Me
Persnickety
Petite Ballet
Puddin
Siloam Baby Talk
Siloam Bye Lo
Siloam June Bug
Siloam Little Girl
Siloam Pink Petite
Stella de Oro

Double Miniatures

Lady Limelight
Little Red Dazzler
Mini Pearl

Spiders and Near-Spiders

Aabachee
Atlas
Blue Orchid
Celestial Light
Dark Star
Dervish
Down South
Ferris Wheel
Flycatcher
Garden Portrait
Gentle Breeze
Green Avalanche
Green Spider
Green Tarantula
Green Widow
Greta
Ice Carnival
Kindly Light
Lily Dache
Mabel Fuller
Mister Big
Monster
Parfait
Scorpio
Spencer Fuller
Spindazzle
Stoplight

Giant Blooms

Beaming Light
Border Giant
Chicago Royal Robe
Chinese Son
Christopher Columbus
Decatur Moonlight
Downing Street
Emerald Dew
Flaming Delight
Grand Opera
Holiday Delight
Hot Toddy
Hudson Valley
Lake Norman Sunset
Mauna Loa
Molokai
Nicholas
Olive Bailey Langdon
Paul Bunyan
Pink Swan
Prairie Moonlight
Right On
Rosy Image
Royal Hermitage
Shola
Sombrero Way
Spring Chimes
Sunrise Melody
Sunrise Serenade
Susan Elizabeth
Thelma Monette
Thunder Clap
Washingtons Farewell
When I Dream
Wide Wide World
Wild Era
Wild Lemonade

Appendix

The American Hemerocallis Society

NO MATTER WHAT your favorite horticultural interest might be, you can probably find a national organization for it. Plant societies exist for everything from azaleas to wildflowers and from Christmas trees to penstemons. Each association encourages the growing of a particular genus of plant and promotes research in developing and registering better cultivars. Its members exchange and publish cultural information and many become involved in such activities as meetings, shows, and garden tours.

Daylily lovers are fortunate to have an excellent group — the American Hemerocallis Society. This thriving advocate for daylilies got its start in the Midwest with a radio program, the Garden Club of the Air, which was broadcast daily for twenty-seven years and hosted by Helen Field Fischer, sister of the well-known nurseryman, Henry Field. Mrs. Fischer loved daylilies and frequently praised them on her program. Thanks to her question-and-answer format,

many area gardeners got to know each other and formed the Hemerocallis Round Robin, an exchange of ideas by mail. It was inevitable that eventually someone would organize a gathering of *Hemerocallis* gardeners, and in July, 1946, the first such event was held in Shenandoah, Iowa. The gathering was a huge success. Thanks to radio publicity, daylily fans arrived by the hundreds in cars, trains, and buses from all over the Midwest.

Realizing that the time had come to take advantage of all the excitement about daylilies, a group of enthusiasts organized the Midwest Hemerocallis Society, and to their surprise, gardeners from the rest of the country were soon clamoring to join. The first year, 757 members paid annual dues of $3 to join. By the following year the group included members from forty-three states as well as England and Canada. In order to become less regional, in 1949 the name of the group was changed to the Hemerocallis

Society, and later to the American Hemerocallis Society.

As interest in daylilies increased, many regional organizations were formed, and at present there are twenty-one such groups; some of these are comprised of several small states: Region 4, for instance, consists of seven states, including all of New England and New York. Region 5, on the other hand, consists only of the state of Georgia. Members automatically become members of the regional group in their area.

The AHS holds a convention near an outstanding daylily-growing area each summer. The regional groups hold their own conventions, organize tours and flower shows during the blooming season, and meet for lectures and slide or video shows at other times of the year. Many members have display gardens that are open to the public at certain times during the blooming season.

Much of the work of the national society is involved with the registration of new daylilies and in giving awards for outstanding cultivars. It maintains an elaborate system of classifying and registering cultivars — over 32,000 to date — and adds several hundred new ones each year. The society also maintains a membership list of several thousand people, including many from foreign countries. In addition, the society publishes various informational booklets, directories of the registered cultivars, and directories of members; and they rent slides and videos of impressive quality.

Another of the society's activities is to organize a popularity contest each fall, whereby each member is asked to vote for ten favorite daylily cultivars. The result is a list of the 100 most popular, published in the *Daylily Journal* every winter (see Chapter 13). The popularity list and the listing of various award winners are important to the industry. Both are often quoted in garden magazines and catalogs and greatly influence which cultivars customers will be requesting at garden outlets, and therefore, the selection of plants that nurseries will offer for sale.

One of the things we like best about belonging to the American Hemerocallis Society is its quarterly magazine, *The Daylily Journal*, which has many high-quality, full-color photos of new daylilies and outstanding gardens. Included are stories of hybridizers and their successes, cultural information, dates of upcoming events, and lists of award-winning cultivars. Leading daylily nurseries advertise their wares in the journal, and the best-known hybridizers often make the first offers of their originations there. The Journal also offers tips on how to form local daylily clubs and plan activities, since the regional groups often cover such large areas that members find it difficult to get together.

A particularly enjoyable feature of the journal is the "Round Robin" column, a holdover from the earliest days of the society. Here you can read first-hand experiences about growing various kinds of daylilies as well as opinions about fertilizers, pesticides, new cultivars, blooming times, plant hardiness, and hybridizing methods.

No lover of daylilies needs a society to enjoy growing daylilies, but, at the risk of sounding like a commercial for the American Hemerocallis Society, we recommend that if you have more than a passing interest in daylilies, it is very worthwhile to become a member. It is likely to add to your enjoyment of growing the world's most beautiful flowers.

MEMBERSHIP in the American Hemerocallis Society includes the *Daylily Journal* four times a year and membership in the regional group. Individual, family, and life memberships are available. The present address is: The American Hemerocallis Society, Elly Launius, Executive Secretary, 1454 Rebel Drive, Jackson, MS 39211. The present individual annual dues are $18.00.

The following booklets are available from the American Hemerocallis Society:

Welcome to the World of Daylilies.

Everything You've Always Wanted to Know about Daylilies

Membership List and By-laws

Hemerocallis Check List of Named Cultivars 1957-1973

Hemerocallis Check List of Named Cultivars 1973-1983

Hemerocallis Check List of Named Cultivars 1983-1988

Judges Handbook

The Art of Hybridizing

Some Basic Hemerocallis Genetics

The Elusive Blue Daylily

Landscaping with Daylilies

(If you are not a member, write to the above address for more information and prices.)

Slides and videos are available for rent to members. Write Donna Sylvester, Slide Librarian, 1221 Highway 7 N., Tonasket, WA 98855.

Regional Districts of the American Hemerocallis Society

Region One—Iowa, Minnesota, Nebraska, North Dakota, South Dakota

Region Two—Illinois, Indiana, Michigan, Ohio, Wisconsin

Region Three—Delaware, District of Columbia, Maryland, New Jersey, Pennsylvania, Virginia, West Virginia

Region Four— Connecticut, Maine, Massachusetts, New Hampshire, New York, Rhode Island, Vermont

Region Five—Georgia

Region Six—New Mexico, Texas

Region Seven—Arizona, California, Nevada

Region Eight—Oregon, Washington

Region Nine—Colorado, Idaho, Montana, Utah, Wyoming

Region Ten—Kentucky, Tennessee

Region Eleven—Kansas, Missouri, Oklahoma

Region Twelve—Florida

Region Thirteen—Arkansas, Louisiana

Region Fourteen—Alabama, Mississippi

Region Fifteen—North and South Carolina

Books of Interest to Daylily Growers

Daylilies, by A. B. Stout. Originally printed by Macmillan in 1934. Reprinted by Sagapress, Inc., in 1986 and distributed by R. and P. Kraus, Route 100, Millwood, NY 10546

> *A thorough history of the evolution of daylilies, including descriptions and colored pictures of species, varieties, and many of the earliest cultivars. Includes some cultural information.*

Daylily Encyclopedia, edited by Steve Webber, 1988, distributed by Webber Gardens, 9180 Main St., Damascus, MD 20872.

> *Excellent information about daylily forms, bloom sequence, modern miniatures, awards, and a helpful list of the names and descriptions of 1,000 popular daylily cultivars.*

Hemerocallis: The Daylily, by R. W. Munson, Jr., Timber Press, 1989.

> *Beautiful colored pictures and excellent information make this book an important addition to the library. Includes special information on daylily breeding, including the history of daylily breeding beginning where the Stout book leaves off, much information about how cultivars are judged, and the awards they receive. Fine descriptions and illustrations, especially for many evergreen cultivars, make this book especially useful to southern gardeners and hybridizers.*

Daylily Nurseries

(Some charge a small fee for their catalogs; some have slides and videos for rent)

Ater Daylilies
3803 Greyatone Dr.
Austin, TX 78731

Barnee's Gardens
Route 10, Box 2010
Nacogdoches
TX 75961

Balash Gardens
26595 H. Drive North
Albion, MI 49224

Big Tree Daylily
  Garden
777 Gen. Hutchinson
  Pkwy.
Longwood, FL 32750

Lee Bristol Nursery
Gaylordsville
CT 06755
208)

Busse Gardens
Route 2, Box 238
Cokato, MN 55321

Coburg Planting
  Fields
573 E. 600 North
Valparaiso, IN 46383

Daylily Discounters
Route 2, Box 24
Alachua, FL 32615

Daylily World
P. O. Box 1612
Sanford, FL 32772

Floyd Cove Nursery
11 Shipyard Lane
Setkauket, NY 11733
(516)
Four Winds Garden
P. O. Box 141
So. Harpswell
ME 04079

Galloway Gardens
3412 Galloway
Jackson, MS 39216

Guidry's Daylily
  Garden
1005 E. Vermilion St.
Abbeville, LA 70510

IRONGATE
KINGS MT.

Mrs. Ralph Henry
616 So. College   501) 524-5242
Siloam Springs
AR 72761

Hillside Daylily
  Garden
14 Linden Hill Dr.
Crescent Springs
KY 41017

Howard J. Hite
370 Gallogly Rd.
Pontiac, MI 48055

Jackson and Perkins
1 Rose Lane
Medford, OR 97501

Joiner Gardens
33 Romney Place
Wymberly
GA 31406

Klehm Nursery
Route 5, Box 197
Penny Rd.
So. Barrington
IL 60010

Meadowlake
  Gardens
Route 4, Box 709
Walterboro
SC 29488

Mercers Garden
6215 Maude St.
Fayetteville
NC 28306

Oakes Daylilies
8204 Monday Rd.
Corryton, TN 37721

Saxton Gardens
1 First St.
Saratoga Springs
NY 12866

Scott Daylily Farm
5830 Clark Rd.
Harrison, TN 37341

Seawright Gardens
134 Indian Hill
Carlisle, MA 01741

Spring Creek Daylily
  Garden
25150 Gosling
Spring, TX 77389

Dave Talbott
4038 Highway 17
  South
Green Cove
FL 32043

Thundering Springs
  Daylily Garden
P. O. Box 2013
Dublin, GA 31040

Tranquil Lake
  Nursery Inc.
45 River St.
Rehoboth, MA 02769

Wayside Gardens
Hodges, SC 29653

White Flower Farm
Litchfield, CT 06759

Gilbert H. Wild and
  Son, Inc.
Sarcoxie, MO 64862

Wimberlyway
  Gardens
7024 NW 18th Ave.
Gainesville, FL 32605

Windmill Gardens
P. O. Box 351
Luverne, AL 36049

Sources of Supplies

Ken Durio
Route 7, Box 43
Opelousas,
LA 70570

Lanolin paste

Eon Industries
3002 Manley Road
Maumee
OH 43537

Metal plant labels

Evergreen
P.O. Box 922
Cloverdale
CA 95425

Plant labels

Forestlake Gardens
Box 535
Locust Grove
VA 22508

*Tetraploid and diploid
seeds, also colchicine*

Gardener's Supply
128 Intervale Road
Burlington
VT 05401

*Supplies, labels, rooting
compounds, unusual
equipment*

A. M. Leonard, Inc.
6665 Spiker Road
P.O. Box 81,
Piqua, OH 45356

*Labels, stakes, tools,
equipment*

Park Seed Co.
Cokesbury Road
Greenwood, SC
29647-0001

*Daylily seeds, grow lights,
and garden supplies*

Glossary

Anther. Top of stamen that contains the pollen.

Asexual reproduction. The propagation of a plant by cuttings, division, grafts, layers, tissue culture, or other vegetative means, rather than by seeds.

Auxin. A hormone that controls plant growth.

Back-cross. Term used in hybridization that means the crossing of a seedling with one of its parents.

Band. A color marking on daylily segments above the throat of the flower.

Bare-rooted. A plant that is transplanted without soil attached to its roots.

Bicolor. A flower with light-colored outer segments and dark-colored inner segments. In a *Reverse bicolor*, the outer segments are darker, and the inner ones, lighter.

Bitone. Flower with inner and outer segments of different hues of the same color.

Bract. A leaf on the scape from which a flower often arises.

Border. A flower bed, usually consisting of a variety of plants.

Bud builder. A daylily that continues to produce buds after it has started to bloom and therefore flowers over a long season.

Calyx. The outermost group of floral parts.

Chimera. A plant consisting of mixed diploid and polyploid tissues, often the result of not having been completely converted to a tetraploid. Such plants are usually not stable and should be observed for some time before being introduced or used in breeding.

Chromosome. Minute parts of a cell containing the genes. Diploid daylilies contain twenty-two chromosomes; triploids, thirty-three; and tetraploids, forty-four.

Clone. New plant that has been reproduced asexually and has characteristics identical to those of the parent. Recently the term has been frequently used in connection with tissue culture.

Colchicine. An alkaloid, derived from the autumn crocus, used in creating tetraploids.

Cold frame. An outdoor seed or plant bed enclosed by a frame with a removable transparent cover. It is intended for growing plants in a protected environment with no artificial heat.

Compost. Nutrient-rich, partially decomposed organic matter that is excellent for building up worn-out soil.

Cross-pollination. The pollination of one plant by another.

Crown. The part of a plant where the foliage and roots meet.

Cultivar. Named variety of a plant that is different from the species and usually an improvement over it. Cultivars of daylilies, like those of most plants, do not come true from seed, and it is necessary to propagate them by asexual means.

Diploid. In daylilies, each diploid plant cell has twenty-two chromosomes, except the seed producing cells, which have only eleven. Most daylilies are diploids.

Diurnal. A daylily flower that opens in the morning or during the day.

Division. The splitting apart of a daylily clump into two or more pieces in order to start new plants or to keep the plant healthy.

Dominant. In hybridizing, those characteristics that dominate the recessive ones in a new hybrid.

Dormancy. The rest period of a plant during which it is not growing or showing signs of life. Also refers to the state of seeds before they sprout.

Dormant. Refers to a class of daylilies that are deciduous. All growth stops in the late fall and the leaves die.

Double. Daylily flowers with more than the usual six segments (three petals and three sepals).

Evergreen. A class of daylily with foliage that stays green all winter in the South, although in northern climates it is likely to turn brown. Evergreens are usually regarded as less hardy than the dormants.

Eye or eyezone. A distinct color marking above the throat of a daylily. A halo is less distinct than an eye.

Genes. Parts of the chromosome that carry the hereditary characteristics.

Germination. The sprouting of seeds.

Halo. See *Eye*.

Harden off. The process whereby perennials and annuals that have been started indoors are gradually exposed to outside conditions.

Herbicide. A chemical used for killing unwanted plants, or to prevent weed seeds in the ground from sprouting.

Hybrid. A plant cultivar developed by the cross-pollination of two plants that are genetically different.

Insecticide. A chemical for killing insects.

Line crossing. In hybridizing, the crossing of seedlings of the same parents with each other.

Magnesium. A trace element needed in small amounts for good daylily growth.

Mature plant. A plant that is old enough to produce blooms and seeds.

Miniature. A daylily with blooms less than 3 inches in diameter.

Miticide. A chemical for killing mites.

Mutant. An offspring which, even though it was produced asexually, differs markedly from its parent in some way.

Nocturnal. A daylily whose flowers open sometime during the early evening or night and depending on when it opens, closes between late morning and early afternoon the next day.

Offshoot or offset. A small plant growing from the main stem of a plant, just under the ground. Often forms roots and can be severed from the parent and grown into a new plant.

Outcrossing. In hybridizing, the crossing of a seedling to an unrelated cultivar or species.

Ova. The female part of the flower that develops into a seed.

Petal. The outer parts (segments) of a flower that show the color. A typical daylily flower has six segments. The three inner ones are petals, and the three outer are sepals

pH. The alkalinity-acidity condition of the soil. Most garden soils range from 5 (acid) to 7 (neutral), and the majority of daylilies grow well within this latitude, although they appear to do best in a soil of pH 5½ to 7.

Pistil. The female reproductive organ of a flower. It consists of a green tube in the center of the stamens and sticks out beyond them. The top is called a *stigma*.

Pollen. The dustlike particles produced by the male stamens in a flower. Daylily pollen grains are usually red, brown, or yellow in color and are spread from flower to flower by insects, hybridizers, or occasionally by the wind.

Pollination. The fertilization of the female ova of a plant by the transfer of pollen either from the male portion of a flower to the female pistil of the same flower (self-pollination) or between two different flowers (cross-pollination), usually resulting in a seed. Hybridizers cross-pollinate plants to create new cultivars.

Polychrome. Flowers of a blend of many colors.

Polyploid. A plant with more than the usual set of chromosomes in each cell, except those of the pollen and ova.

Proliferation. A leafy shoot that occasionally forms on the scape of a daylily about the time it blooms. It can be removed, rooted, and grown into a new plant identical to the parent.

Rebloomer. A plant that blooms during its normal period and then, after resting awhile, produces a second set of buds and blossoms.

Recessive. The characteristics of a plant that are subordinate to the dominant characteristics during the breeding process. Recessive characteristics often reappear in the next generation, however.

Reverse bicolor. See *Bicolor*.

Rooting chemical. A chemical in powder or liquid form that is used to treat a proliferation to stimulate faster root development.

Scape. The leafless stalk on which the flowers of plants such as daylilies are produced.

Seedling. In daylilies, this term refers to an unnamed plant that has been grown from seed.

Segment. In a typical daylily flower, the segments consist of three inner petals and three outer sepals; doubles have more.

Selection. The choosing of the best plants from a group of seedlings for further breeding or possible registration. Also refers to a seedling that has been chosen and numbered but not yet named or registered.

Self. A daylily with petals and sepals of the same color. The throat may be a different color, however.

Selfing or self-pollination. The crossing of a bisexual plant with itself or another plant of the same cultivar.

Semi-evergreen. Refers to a class of daylilies with foliage that goes dormant in the late fall only on top in the South, leaving 3 to 4 inches of green. In the North, the foliage dies and the plant becomes dormant.

Sepal. The calyx or leaflike back row of flower segments behind the main showy petals. These may be of the same or of a different color than the petals. See *Petal*.

Shade. A lower degree of sunlight. Light shade usually refers to a few hours of morning or late afternoon sun but considerable skylight all day long. Moderate shade indicates filtered light such as that coming through trees with light foliage, but little or no direct sunlight at any time. Heavy shade occurs under trees with dense foliage, and such locations are suitable for only a few plant species. Light afternoon shade brings out the best color in some of the red- and pink-flowering daylilies.

Spider. A daylily with long, narrow petals. A length-to-width ratio of 5 to 1 has been suggested as the qualification for a "true" spider, but this rule has seldom been strictly followed.

Stamen. The male part of the flower that produces the pollen. A daylily has six, each consisting of a stem with a pollen-covered anther on top.

Sterile. The inability of a plant to produce fertile pollen or to accept it.

Stigma. The sticky top of the pistil that receives the pollen.

Stolon. Underground root that spreads away from the parent plant and forms a new plant at its tip.

Stoloniferous. Refers to a plant that produces stolons.

Systemics. Chemicals that a plant absorbs through its roots and leaves and that permeate the entire plant. Some kinds of insecticides, herbicides, and fungicides are systemic.

Tetraploid. A tetraploid daylily has forty-four chromosomes (four sets) in each cell, except the pollen and ova cells, each of which have half that number.

Tissue culture. The asexual propagation, or cloning, of plants by the rapid increase of cell growth under sterile, carefully controlled conditions of temperature, nutrients, and pH in a laboratory.

Trace element. An element essential in small amounts for good plant growth.

Turgid. A term used to describe a plant that is adequately supplied with water. Cuttings from turgid plants root better. Seedlings and mature plants can be transplanted more safely if they are turgid.

Variegated. Green foliage that is marked with yellow or white streaks or blotches.

Variety. This term is often used interchangeably with cultivar, or named plant, but botanically it refers only to the named strains of native species.

Viability. The ability of a seed to germinate.

Cultivar Index

Numbers in italics, such as *35*, indicate that illustrations appear on that page.

General Index

Numbers in italics, such as *35*, indicate that illustrations appear on that page.